Feeling Wisdom

Also by Rob Preece

The Courage to Feel: Buddhist Practices for
    Opening to Others

Preparing for Tantra: Creating the Psychological
    Ground for Practice

The Psychology of Buddhist Tantra

The Wisdom of Imperfection: The Challenge of
    Individuation in Buddhist Life

feeling wisdom

Working with Emotions Using Buddhist Teachings and Western Psychology

Rob Preece

SHAMBHALA
Boston & London
2014

Shambhala Publications, Inc.
Horticultural Hall
300 Massachusetts Avenue
Boston, Massachusetts 02115
www.shambhala.com

9 8 7 6 5 4 3 2 1
First Edition

Printed in the United States of America
⊗ This edition is printed on acid-free paper that meets the
American National Standards Institute Z39.48 Standard.
♻ This book is printed on 30% postconsumer recycled paper.
For more information please visit www.shambhala.com.
Distributed in the United States by Penguin Random House LLC
and in Canada by Random House of Canada Ltd

Designed by K. E. White

Library of Congress Cataloging-in-Publication Data

Preece, Rob, author.
Feeling wisdom: working with emotions using Buddhist teachings and
western psychology / Rob Preece.—First edition.
pages cm
Includes bibliographical references.
ISBN 978-1-61180-168-2 (alk. paper)
1. Buddhism—Psychology. 2. Emotions—Religious aspects—Buddhism.
I. Title.
BQ4570.P76P73 2014
294.3′44—dc23
2014011587

Contents

Acknowledgments

I WISH TO DEDICATE THIS WORK to all of those people who
have opened their lives to me and shared their vulnerabilities
and their emotional struggles throughout the past twenty-five
years of my work as a psychotherapist. I offer my gratitude for
their trust and their dedication to the journey they embarked
upon. I have learned so much through them. I would also like
to offer my gratitude to my wife, Anna, whose natural wisdom
in relation to the world of feeling has always been a source of
insight and inspiration. Her experience of working with the
body through movement is an invaluable addition to the text.
Lastly, I would like to dedicate this work to my root teacher,
Lama Thubten Yeshe, who passed away in 1984 and whose
understanding of and compassion for the complexity of Western emotional life was an extraordinary guiding light.

Introduction

POSSIBLY THE SINGLE STRONGEST motivating factors in
our lives are our feelings. We can see this on the level of strong
emotions like anger or subtler feelings of care and compassion. Whether we are able to be aware of these feelings and
live in relation to them or whether they drive us unconsciously
depends on the individual. They are in any case there in our
body. For most of us the way we learn to live with our emotional and feeling life arises in a relatively arbitrary way. I was
certainly never given any guidance when I was at school or
growing up regarding how to cope with strong emotions and
feelings. Unfortunately, there was something of a taboo, for a
man in the United Kingdom, around expressing feelings, and
so I felt they needed to be held in and potentially suppressed.

When I became involved in Tibetan Buddhism at a young age some forty years ago, one of my hopes was that it would offer me a way of both understanding and working with my emotional life. What I found was that within the world of Buddhist thinking, there are contrasting views around the subject of feeling and emotion and how we are supposed to deal with them or work with them. There is one view that sees feelings and emotions as something that should be controlled and overcome because they are the root of suffering. Then there is another perspective that sees emotions as the source of transformation. It is often because of problems with our emotional life that some of us study Buddhist ideas and meditation practices that might offer a kind of panacea—but is it that simple?

One of my reasons for engaging with Buddhist practice was that I often suffered periods of depression and anxiety when I was in my twenties. I found that Buddhist thinking gave some valuable answers that were often of an existential nature. Its recognition of the root of suffering in the way we grasp at a sense of self was radical for me at the time. What I needed to find, however, was a way of actually addressing and dealing directly with strong emotional states such as depression. I spent many years studying profound teachings on Buddhist philosophy, psychology, and what is known as "mind training," and yet I did not feel that what I was experiencing psychologically was really being addressed. While many of these teachings provided a significant cognitive, intellectual understanding of Buddhist psychology, I still seemed unable to resolve the more painful and complex aspects of my emotional life. I found myself in a place of some conflict because I felt that within my study of Buddhist philosophy, I had begun to place all feelings and emotions in one bag as things that needed to be pacified because they give rise to suffering.

It was during a period of retreat that I began to discover a different Buddhist approach that did provide a means of working with my emotional life and with the depressions I experienced. This was an approach that went beneath my conceptual, intellectual knowledge and related more directly to my experience, exemplified by the practice known as Mahamudra, which was taught me by my teacher Lama Thubten Yeshe. This practice from the Tibetan tradition has many similarities to what is now familiar in the West as the practice of mindfulness. Mahamudra specifically leads us to rest in a state of present awareness, the natural clarity of the mind. Within this state of clear, present awareness, I began to live with painful feelings in a way that actually helped for the first time. I found myself able to witness feelings without drowning in their power. My relationship to feelings became much more open, accepting, and less of a struggle.

When I later began to train as a psychotherapist, I found another level of insight into the nature of feeling and emotion that became very important to me alongside this Buddhist approach. This was the view that recognized that my feeling life was part of a psychological process that needed to be given certain conditions to unfold. There was also the recognition that our emotions often have origins earlier in life that need to be explored more deeply. Recognizing the psychological wounds that contribute to our emotional life then helps a healing process to unfold. While it is clear that some therapeutic approaches are more effective than others, what they all offer is an appreciation of and respect for the subtleties of an individual's emotional process. What I have subsequently come to see is that it is a combination of Eastern Buddhist and Western psychological understanding in practice that really helps with the complexity of our psychological nature and the transformation of emotions. It has led me to follow what might then be called a contemplative style of psychotherapy that combines aspects of both meditation and reflection.

In the West we could be seen as very dominated by our emotions, and if we compare ourselves with the Tibetans, for example, this would certainly seem to be the case. As I lived among the Tibetans for many years, I was surprised to discover that they do not relate to questions of feeling in the same way that we do. There seems to be no word in Tibetan that is an actual equivalent to *emotion,* and the term Tibetans use for *feeling* does not have the same connotations as ours or convey the same sense. It does not seem to be important to ask a Tibetan how he or she feels about something. This seems to be a psychological territory that has far greater significance to us in the West, where the nature of our feeling life has, for good or ill, become so important.

I was partly prompted to write this book when I began to see that some Tibetan teachers actually think that being in touch with our feelings may be doing us Westerners more harm than good.[1] It may be true that in the West we are more governed by our feeling and emotional life than Tibetans are, but having spent a considerable amount of my adult life trying to get in touch with my feelings, I found this view very confusing. What I began to consider is that we are looking across a divide that has more to do with East-West cultural and psychological differences than with Buddhism itself. There is within the Tibetan Buddhist world, partly because of language, a tendency to conflate feeling and emotion into one package in a way that can cause us to see all emotion as delusion and affliction. Perhaps we can consider that Tibetans do not "do" feelings as we do in the West; they have their own cultural way with their feeling life, and it is very different from ours. Fortunately, there is a growing number of Tibetan teachers, and I include His Holiness the Dalai Lama among them, who are really looking at the way we use the term *emotion* in the West and at how we may need to bring Buddhist knowledge together with modern psychological understanding.

It may nevertheless be useful to ask the question, "Do feelings matter?" And from my experience as both a psychotherapist and a meditator, it would seem they most certainly do. At the heart of this question is a potential confusion in the way we use the terms *feeling* and *emotion* to cover a spectrum of experiences. As a Buddhist, this confusion is compounded by the fact that there is no word for emotion in Tibetan, and the word for feeling is used slightly differently. There is an important distinction between emotion and feeling and also between feeling as a physical tone of an experience that includes sensation and feeling as a way of evaluating or knowing about the world. When I ask myself how I felt about the tsunami in Japan, I am aware of feelings of horror, shock, awe, and huge compassion. When I consider the way reckless practices in the banking world have allowed people to become extremely rich at the expense of millions, I feel anger and outrage. When I feel hunger at the end of the day and delight in the flavors of a good curry, I am filled with pleasure. All of these different feelings demonstrate a huge range of responses. They are not all of the same order. They are not merely delusions to be abandoned because they are the basis of suffering. There is a spectrum of feelings that can be important responses to situations and experiences without which our life would be sterile and unfeeling. My compassion for the people of Japan is a strong feeling that is at the heart of Buddhism. My sense of horror and shock may be an important way of assessing the nature of people's difficulties. My anger and outrage at the banks is based on a deep ethical feeling that knows something is not right. My feeling of hunger and the pleasure of eating are natural responses to my body and its sensory capacity.

The founder of analytical psychology, C. G. Jung, said that without the "feeling function," as he called it, we would have no discernment of an ethical or moral gauge. When we speak of feeling in this sense, it is not the experience of affect but, rather, a subtle evaluation process that goes on at a level beneath the conceptual mind. Within Buddhist understanding, the most fundamental experience of feeling arises in relation to our sensory contact with the world and is also a very basic and raw evaluation of what is pleasant, unpleasant, or neutral. What we have to learn in our life is to discern the differences between these levels and modes of feeling so that we can recognize those occasions when we are in touch with some important knowledge about our experience and those when we are just caught in reactive affect.

Feeling and our entire feeling life can actually bring with it a great source of insight and wisdom. It is a reference point through which we can evaluate the world that sometimes warns us of dangers. It is a way of being in relationship to our experiences that enables us to develop important and significant feelings such as compassion, love, concern, care, and so on. If we can learn to be with our feeling reality, it will ultimately begin to open us to the deepest level of felt experience, which is intimately tied up with the innate nature of mind.

In Buddhist understanding the mind's true nature is essentially clear and free of defilement even though it is obscured by our psychological and emotional life. But this innate primordial mind, or clear-light mind, as it is sometimes called, has two dimensions. One is a significant aspect of mind that is a natural clarity and wisdom awareness that recognizes the true nature of reality. But this experience has a feeling tone intimately associated with it that is present because it is intrinsic to the very nature of primordial mind. This intrinsic nature of mind is therefore described as the inseparable union of clarity, or wisdom, with the feeling of bliss. In the Tibetan tradition there is a particular emphasis on the feeling of bliss, but this could equally be love, compassion, and joy, which are some of its natural tones.

So in our spiritual journey we try to bring together a profound insight into the nature of reality but also a deep awakening of feeling. Feeling is not something that we should dismiss or disregard in favor of mind. As Westerners we may be considerably more entangled in our emotions than are those in the East, but it is nonetheless our feeling life that needs to be understood and, indeed, transformed and awakened. This means that the practice of meditation needs to bring us into relationship with the emotional life that we need to transform. It will also bring us into relationship with deeper, subtle levels of felt experience that tell us a great deal about our relationship to life. More deeply, we will come to experience a quality of feeling that has profound meaning to it. The qualities of love, compassion, joy, and, ultimately, bliss are all within our nature. We may be able to develop wisdom through meditation, but without the feeling dimension, that can be arid. It is often said in Buddhist teachings that in our life we need the two wings of a bird: one is wisdom and the other is a feeling of compassion and love.

In this book I wish to look at ways in which we can live with our feeling life that will begin to bring to light the wisdom that lies within it, drawing on both Buddhist and Western approaches. For many of us, feelings and emotions are the root of so much of our suffering, but equally they can be the ground of our awakening. It is sometimes said that we can experience happiness only if we truly embrace our pain. To lose relationship to feeling would be to become barren and dry. In discussing the feeling reality, I wish to differentiate the notions of delusion, emotion, feeling, and felt sense and to explore the distinction between emotions and what are sometimes called destructive emotions. These are all important considerations if we are to live more comfortably with our emotional life and gain insight and wisdom. I wish to draw on my own psychotherapeutic background as well as the work of people such as John Welwood, the psychotherapist and writer, and others in the West who have brought together Eastern and Western understanding. I will touch on Jung's "feeling function" and look at some of the traditional Buddhist views on this subject. In part 1 I will be exploring and mapping the territory of our feeling life, drawing on Buddhist and Western perspectives. In part 2 I will be looking at some of the important ingredients in and ways of transforming our emotional life, and in part 3 I will be looking at the quality of feeling as it unfolds into its wisdom nature.

Feeling is the source of so much wisdom if we know how to live with it. Ultimately, it is the deepest level of feeling—universal compassion and bliss, conjoined with wisdom realizing the nature of reality—that becomes a buddha's awakened experience. This is the same "stuff" as our current day-to-day feelings; it is just a refined and more illuminated aspect of it. Our feelings and emotions are the raw material of our awakening. If we disregard them, we miss a vital resource.

Part One

feeling
awareness

I

life's blood

I T COULD BE SAID THAT our capacity to feel is one of the
most significant aspects of our state of being. Whether it
is the subtle, soft nuances of calm when we are sitting in a
quiet place in the country; the explosive eruptions of outrage
when we are hurt; or the passion we feel in what we do, our
feeling life is rich and continuous. So long as we are awake, we
are going to have waves of feelings throughout the course of
our day. Some of these may be pleasant and satisfactory and
may not disturb us unduly; others may be unpleasant and distressing. How we live with this continuous flux is dependent
upon our own capacity and the degree of intensity of feeling
we experience. Our feeling life is a richness that enlivens our
life, but it can also be a torment that brings continual pain.

Without the capacity to feel we would not be able to recognize the subtle nuances of our life, its tones and shades, its beauty and its pain. Because our feeling capacity is grounded in the body it has a strong relationship to our capacity for sensation, and these two are intimately connected. Feeling is our lifeblood and so long as we are alive it will enrich and imbue everything we do and all of our relationships.

Imagine, however, waking in the morning, turning on the hot water and watching it stream out, then placing your hand in the water and feeling nothing. Imagine putting food into your mouth and feeling and tasting nothing, as some experience who have had a severe stroke. There is no basis of pleasant or unpleasant feelings. If a pet dog that had been a constant and cherished companion were to die and we felt nothing we may wonder about our emotional well-being. If one of my children were injured and I felt no response it would be of serious concern. If we had no response of feeling or sensation within our experiences we would be living an utterly different existence.

Feeling is so fundamental to our existence that we cannot avoid the fact that to cope with our life we must learn to relate to it in a meaningful and healthy way. According to the Buddha's teachings on dependent origination as described within the wheel of life, feeling is the seventh link.[1] It is the moment when, once we make contact through our senses with the appearances of reality, we begin to feel. It is this feeling that moves us to act throughout our life. We respond to feeling, which in turn gives rise to the movement toward or away from what we encounter. In the evolution of stages depicted in the wheel of life, we might consider that if we could break this link, we would be free, we would no longer be caught in the cycle of suffering. But does this mean we have to avoid feeling?

I recall living with a group of fellow Buddhist practitioners in a community many years ago. Among us there was a view that one of the ways to free ourselves from suffering and the distractions of both pleasant and unpleasant feelings was to "avoid contact with the object." This curious phrase led me to believe that I needed to abandon the things that I did that would lead to feelings that arise from contact with enjoyable objects. I gave away my guitar and all the other musical instruments I possessed because they were objects I might enjoy. There were many of us who believed relationships, in particular, were something to be avoided because this kind of contact would lead to all manner of feelings that were disturbing and would be a distraction to our practice of the dharma. It was a great source of amusement that while we tried to live relatively celibate lives, we had in the building one room with a double bed where couples could go to have "contact with the object." I cannot imagine what we were thinking.

When I look back at those times, I am shocked at our naïveté. Did I really believe that I could avoid contact with things that would give rise to feeling? The problem was, as always, not the objects nor the contact nor specifically the feelings. It was the next link in the process, the eighth link in the twelve links of interdependent arising, namely that of craving and grasping. It is true that in the twelve links illustrated in paintings of the wheel of life, the link of feeling is depicted by a man with an arrow in his eye. But this does not mean that all feeling is suffering. Feeling does, however, lead to the tendency to grasp at some feelings as pleasurable and to push others away as painful.

When we contract around our feelings and make them fixed and solid, we turn our pleasures into caca, as Lama Yeshe once put it. Similarly, when we tighten around our discomfort and pain, we turn it into suffering. Feelings are not the problem, and yet we may spend a lot of time trying to avoid them. They make us open and vulnerable, and this is not always what we wish for. Even the good feelings we encounter may threaten us because we open to them, and this can lead to something we cannot bear, namely, separation or loss.

Contact leads to feeling, and separation also leads to feeling. When we come into relationship with another, be it a person or an object, we experience feeling. For some of us this is frightening because it may lead to the pain of separation. Our fear of that pain is then enough to make us avoid relationship. This can happen with another person or with our sense of self. To come into real relationship with our self can be both a great pleasure and a source of love, but it can equally be a source of great pain as we face our wounds. Being out of relationship to our self, however, will be a constant cause for pain. I think it may be important to say that I do not mean by this anything that contradicts the Buddhist notion of emptiness of self; I am referring, rather, to the necessary relative sense of self. Psychologically, this is a self that is crucial to a healthy relationship to the world.

On a deeper level, being out of relationship to our innate nature is also a source of depression, alienation, and lack of meaning that can be unbearable. When we come back into relationship with our innate nature, we will restore a profound feeling of peace, totality, and joy that becomes the ground of our being.

In our spiritual life we may seek an awakening to our innate nature as a quality of wisdom that enables us to see reality differently. We should not overlook the fact that this awakening is not just a mental state; it is also a felt experience. If we have some notion in mind that when we attain an enlightened experience it will be without feeling, we are mistaken. From a Buddhist viewpoint, feeling is known as an ever-present mental factor that accompanies any state of mind. Our feeling experience begins with our present state of being and will be there, albeit in a subtly different way, when we attain the state of awakening. If in meditation we try to separate ourselves from the felt experience, we will be caught in what John Welwood described as spiritual by-passing,[2] where we use our practice to avoid a relationship to feeling.

I have been shocked and surprised when the occasional non-Buddhist friend has made the remark "Of course, you're a Buddhist, you don't have these kinds of feelings" or "You don't have emotional problems." These remarks suggest that there is some popular conception that as Buddhists we do not have feelings or emotions because we have attained some state of detachment. Does detachment mean we no longer feel? If this is the case, then I have no desire to be detached. If I live with the view that my Buddhist practice will gradually elim-inate the presence of feelings, I am mistaken. What it can do is refine my relationship to my feeling life and in the process perhaps enable me to live with the dimension of feeling in a way that is very liberating. It is rather like the way the English continually talk about or, indeed, complain about the weather; perhaps we would like to eliminate weather altogether, but the weather is not the problem. It is our relationship to it that disturbs us.

2

ambivalence
toward feeling

DURING THE PERIOD OF MY training as a psychotherapist, I became increasingly aware of the multitude of
ways in which we respond to our feeling and emotional life.
For many of us it is this side of our life that is the most complex and also the most uncomfortable. What many of us lack
is the capacity or understanding of how to be with our feelings
and emotions, and personally I wish when I was younger that
someone had given me some very basic guidelines. As a man
growing up in the West, I was aware of an ambivalence among
men around our feeling life and was often dismayed at how little we were able to communicate about it. My involvement in
the process of psychotherapy training and entering into therapy gave me an opportunity to learn as never before. I began

to understand that the world of feelings and emotions was not something that was to be feared and avoided, because to do so was fundamentally unhealthy. Within this world of psychotherapy, to be in touch with and begin to explore the underlying process of our emotional life are considered extremely important if we are to resolve our emotional problems.

It was in my early relationship to the Buddhist world that a level of confusion arose around the validity of feelings and emotions, when the general principle I was learning was that the mind's emotional afflictions are to be tamed or overcome. The heroic position of one who does not bow down to emotional afflictions portrayed in texts such as the eighth-century Buddhist monk Shantideva's *Guide to the Bodhisattva's Way of Life* conveyed the idea that I really needed to hold my feelings and emotional responses in check because they were essentially unwholesome.[1] I learned that our emotional life is the driving force behind the actions that then lead to suffering. If we tame this emotional nature of our mind, we will not be driven to create the causes for suffering. What then seems evident within Buddhism generally is that the personal story within our emotional life is not important or significant in the way that it tends to be in the West.

More recently I read an article by an eminent Tibetan lama who said that "being in touch with our feelings could be doing us more harm than good." He also said, "In Asian culture the question 'How are you feeling?' is not asked because of the understanding that the emotions are fickle and changeable."[2] He implied that in the West we take our feelings too seriously and that in Tibet they are recognized to be illusory and are therefore not given much value.

Perhaps this leads me to consider whether we should expect Tibetan teachers to understand and be able to guide us in our emotional and psychological life. After all, they have not grown up in the West with the same kind of psychological pressures we experience. They do not have our kinds of emotional wounding, and they have not been educated in the psychological language of the West. They have their own way of seeing the emotions and a psychological makeup that is culturally very different from our own. A difficulty may arise if we assume they understand and are able to solve our emotional problems.

The seemingly contradictory positions around the nature of feeling and emotion can lead to something of a conflict between what might be considered Buddhist thinking and psychological understanding. Do we allow ourselves to feel or do we not? Do we work through and explore our emotions, or do we control, tame, and overcome them? Do we listen to the personal narrative within our feelings, or is it irrelevant? One thing that has become very clear in both Buddhism and the therapeutic world is that neither the repression of our emotional life nor acting it out resolves or transforms it. Indeed, if we repress our emotions, they will not simply disappear but will become embedded in the body. They may then gradually manifest through our illnesses. If, on the other hand, we become taken over by our emotions and simply act them out, they will perpetuate habits and potentially do great harm to both others and ourselves. What feels important in the exploration of feelings is that we need to bring together a combination of Buddhist and Western understanding in order to address our Western issues regarding our emotional life.

Unfortunately, in the West we do have some ambivalence around our feeling and emotional life. For many of us, to feel is to be alive, awake, and in touch with the world, but sometimes when I see people in the therapeutic space, I encounter those who feel numb and out of touch with any sense of feeling. This can be a dreadfully dead experience, when someone has become so cut off from the feeling connection that she or he feels nothing. This brings a kind of dehumanizing lack of affect in relationship, where the person is so cut off that there is no real contact. When someone experiencing this describes what goes on, there is often a complete lack of the inner feeling tone that gives a strong sense of self. The felt sense of self seems dead or buried, and yet there will remain a kind of mental ego or mental self.

There are those who through some kind of trauma have needed to repress their experience to protect themselves from the intensity of traumatic feelings that may be deep within. With someone who has had to repress in this way, the danger is that all feelings become buried, not just the painful or negative ones. Often someone who has been abused will feel the need to bury positive feelings of care and love because they are just as dangerous as the pain and rage that may be there because of the abuse.

We also live in a world where many people have the tendency to cut themselves off at the neck, so to speak, and remain in the head and the intellect because they are safer and more comfortable. This split from both body and feelings will often lead to a kind of ungrounded or disconnected intellectual response to life that is divorced from feeling and focused on a strong intellectual ego. However, even those who are intellectually eloquent will often sound driven by under-lying emotions when speaking fervently about their views. It is, in this respect, hard to disguise the emotional undercur-rents that live through us. Strong emotions will often erupt through this intellectual defense, and they will shatter its control for a short time until they are discharged.

This more-heady way of being is often related to a lack of relationship to the body such that feeling reality is not acces-sible. This is a tendency that many of us suffer in the West because of the nature of our busy, mind-oriented lifestyles and work. Sitting for hours at a desk in front of computer screens is not particularly conducive to being in touch with the body. It is also often surprising to find that those who are actually quite athletic or who do pursue activities with the body at the gym or in sports can still be remarkably out of touch with the body.

For some the underlying unhappiness and emotional dis-tress within their lives leads to a perpetual need to take refuge in distractions and anesthetics that deaden the feelings. Many do this by using food as a means to push down what is uncom-fortable. For others it can be sensory pleasures: television, alco-hol, work, and even relationships. The ways we lessen the pain and unsatisfactoriness of our life and the feelings it brings can be very sophisticated. Within Buddhist understanding, this kind of relationship to suffering is a central issue that needs to be faced if we are to wake up to our emotional habits.

For many people there is the experience of intense periods of depression that put them in relationship with deep pain and despair that can be completely overwhelming. Unfortu-nately, in our culture there is something of a taboo around openly disclosing that we are feeling depressed. Doing so can often be uncomfortable for others, who don't know how to respond. It can also be accompanied by a sense of shame because we think we should be able to cope. Depression and anxiety can be paralyzing and can often be so hard to bear that the only solution seems to be to find some anesthetic to deaden the pain. Many people turn to medication, which is liberally supported by the medical world's enthusiasm for handing out antidepressant drugs, some of which are, unfortunately, of little value. This is perhaps understandable when a doctor is confronted with patients who are desperate and wish to have rapid relief from their pain.

The strength of darkness, despair, and hopelessness in experiences of depression may be temporarily abated by medication, but seldom does medication resolve the underlying issues. It does, however, require a level of courage and determination to go through depression without anesthetizing the process. I have found in my own journey of depression that I gradually learned to be with the process of descent and reemergence, which I am sure would never have given me the insights it did if I had received medication. My periods of depression, although often desperately painful, were also deeply transformational. What I began to find was that if I could remain with the felt process, I discovered some extraordinary resources within.

Being out of relationship to our feeling life can, unfortunately, be perpetuated by meditation practice if there is a tendency to what John Welwood usefully called spiritual bypassing. We can then enter into mental states of absorption that enable us to dissociate from our feeling and emotional life, giving the illusion that all is well and there are no longer any emotional problems. Regrettably, this state can be perpetuated or even supported by certain styles of practice that become very mind dominated and are divorced from the body and feeling life.

If we consider these various ways of not being in relation to our feeling life, we might also consider the converse. We could become so awash with feeling and emotional affect that it is all we wish to relate to. Unfortunately, there are ways in which we can become addicted to feeling such that there is little capacity to contain or give some kind of boundary to it. Our experience of feeling can be analogous to the qualities of water, we can be flooded with feeling affect that washes through and around every experience. When people become drawn in this way, the sense of separation and boundary can be lost, causing a kind of merging. Feeling in excess without awareness is like gradually sinking into the water and drowning. In the therapeutic context, I have seen this tendency where feelings become overwhelming and the journey is to restore a sense of awareness that can actually raise the head above the water.

Something that has been noticeable with some men in the therapeutic setting, particularly those who are in the therapy world themselves, is a kind of overinfusion of feeling. When we as men—and I can include myself in this—first begin to make deep contact with feeling life, it is like opening the door to a new way of seeing the world. The danger is that we can then become so absorbed in this feeling life that we lose the capacity to contain it: we become enthralled by it. It floods out, and we compulsively want to share our feelings.

This outflow of feeling can become a kind of indulgence that loses the capacity to give feelings a container, allowing them to flood everywhere, just as water will without a container.

So we have two potential directions in which we can go with our feeling life. Repressing it does not help us, nor does flooding the environment with our feelings. Neither of these responses is healthy. It is only when we begin to look at our feeling life in a clearer and more skillful way that we will find a middle ground between these two extremes. To make more sense of this process, however, it is useful to consider the distinction between feeling and emotion on the one hand and what we might recognize as subtler feeling processes on the other.

3

the spectrum
of feeling

O N MANY OCCASIONS DURING the early part of the
monsoon in the Himalayas, I watched with fascination
the emergence of clouds in the clear sky. From the clarity of
blue sky a small wisp of white would suddenly appear. In a
short while it would grow into a small, fluffy white cloud. If
the conditions were right, over time it would gradually swell
into a massive, billowing gray cloud full of power and energy
that flashed and rumbled. Eventually the dark center of this
mass would deposit its contents upon the land below, and following that, I could see its heart collapse. Once the power of
the cloud had been dissipated, it would slowly evaporate away
until once again all that remained was a small wisp drifting in
the vast blue space.

This fascinates me as a metaphor because the emergence of a storm cloud in the early days of the monsoon is so reminiscent of the emergence of strong emotions. What may begin as the wisp of a subtle feeling not yet noticed as anything significant grows into a stronger feeling that starts to draw our attention. Eventually, if the conditions are right, this can become a powerful emotional surge that has the capacity to overwhelm and dominate us as we lose control, driven by its need to express something to dissipate its energy. This may lead us to shower someone with abuse or to burst into tears. Once the core of the emotion has dissipated, the release can enable us to gradually calm down. The remaining feelings can still reverberate around our energy for some time, until eventually they settle back into the ground of our everyday feeling life.

Of course, we need to consider that this entire process is natural and healthy and that problems are present only if we block or distort what is natural. Indeed, we can see that some of our emotional processes are a natural and healthy response, such as grief if someone we are close to dies or anger or outrage if we are abused. We could say that it would be unhealthy not to have these emotions. Other emotional reactions are perhaps more problematic and destructive and may need to be worked with in a way that becomes more healthy.

It is clear, however, that we often, or indeed usually, fail to notice this emotional storm brewing until it reaches a certain level of intensity, by which time we may be totally dominated by the process. If we were more mindful, more aware on a subtle level, we might have noticed what we were beginning to feel when the stirrings of something quite small first began. When we are able to be more present and mindful, we may start to notice the subtle feelings that underlie the strong emotions. We will see that this process can happen slowly, like the gradual buildup of the storm cloud, but often it is very rapid. We have become dominated by strong feelings or emotions before we realize what is going on. Often this occurs in a rush of emotion.

In order to begin to clarify the depths of our feeling life, it is useful to map the territory. As I have implied, our stronger emotions emerge and grow from a feeling base that is not so strongly reactive. Beneath our emotion we are constantly experiencing feelings in relation to our daily experiences. These may ebb and flow, and at any point we may stop and just check in to how we are feeling and notice what is going on. This listening process is familiar to many of us, but for some, actually taking the time to stop and listen in is not familiar at all. As a psychotherapist I am often surprised at the number of people who really do not give themselves the time or space simply to check in. This may be through a lack of familiarity with the process. It may equally be because it is too uncomfortable to do so. There may be deeper emotional distress that it is more comfortable not to feel. For others it is simply that they are so bound up in the head that they are out of touch with their feeling life.

If we give ourselves the time to quieten and settle into our feeling life, we will begin to recognize a spectrum of felt experience that becomes subtler as we go deeper. Eventually, we begin to recognize something far more subtle than even the ebb and flow of our feelings, just as we recognize moisture in the sky only once the cloud has begun to form. In actuality, the sky is blue because of this moisture, which is always there. With our feeling life there is something similar where, as we settle and open within the atmosphere of our felt experience in our body, we will notice an underlying subtle vitality that pervades our awareness. This experience is an ever-present felt quality that remains so long as we are alive. It is the essential felt quality of the mind on an extremely subtle level.

John Welwood put this spectrum of our feeling life into a map that is useful to consider here. He began with the upper level of our emotions; beneath this he placed our feelings, and beneath these he describes what he has called the felt sense, a more diffuse and subtle ground of our feeling life. Below this is what he calls basic aliveness, a subtle level of feeling that is associated with the very vitality of our life.[1]

This map enables us to begin to differentiate clearly our feeling life from our emotional life in terms of its degree of

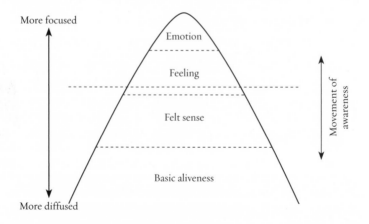

FIG. I. *From John Welwood,* Awakening the Heart *(Boston: Shambhala Publications, 1985), 80.*

intensity and focus. We could say this distinction is a false one, that feeling and emotion are essentially the same. Our emotions, however, are far more intense and focused upon a particular situation. They are more reactive and will dominate our awareness such that they can potentially drown out the surrounding or underlying feeling tone. It is interesting to note that Jung did not use the word *emotion* but, rather, chose to use the term *affect,* reflecting this reactive effect of emotion. Our feelings could then be seen as a subtler movement of our feeling life that can fluctuate and actually contain a multitude of shades at the same time. We may have both positive and negative feelings arising simultaneously that give an experience its particular nuance. For example, there are times when I drive across the moorland where I live and have a deep sense of awe and joy at the sheer beauty of the landscape and sky, and yet I can also feel some tinges of sadness, disappointment, and sometimes anger that the local farmers have set fire to large areas to prevent the spread of a plant called gorse. This mixture of feelings is noticeable if I stop and listen in. If I were to become angry and outraged at the fires, it could drown out the more subtle feelings. As I have indicated on the map above, our level of awareness moves up and down this spectrum, so that we may not always be aware of the more subtle levels of felt experience until we do actually stop and listen.

If we sit and enter a more-contemplative space, we can become aware of the level of what John Welwood calls the felt sense. This more-diffuse level of feeling is centered in the body's natural feeling tone. In Tibetan the word *tsorwa* has a meaning that is not quite "feeling," nor is it just "sensation." It is the felt experience in the body that includes both sensation and feeling. Our unfolding moment-to-moment contact with the experiences of our life brings about a continuous field of feeling/sensation in the body. Our body is the sense organ that is aware of the environment and responds to it constantly with this feeling/sensation tone.

In its most simple sense we experience the sensory world in each moment and discern what is pleasant, unpleasant, or neutral—or we could say, what is safe, unsafe, or neutral. This experience then brings about a more complex process that becomes the basis of stronger feeling and emotion but also moves us to act. This leads us to recognize a spectrum between feeling as an ever-present sensory response and the unfolding of a complex inner feeling reality that is intimately connected to our emotional life. In Buddhist thinking the basic raw level of feeling that discerns what is pleasant, unpleasant, or neutral is seen as the root of our problems because it unconsciously leads us to react to the world through what are called the three poisons of greed, hatred, and ignorance. In this respect we can see feeling as either a cause of our problems or the basis of a profound capacity for discernment, a kind of natural thermometer. How we respond will depend on how we bring awareness to this process.

If we are able to enter into meditation practices that bring us into deeper relationship with the body, we will open up a level of awareness that can increasingly differentiate the subtlest level of this spectrum of feelings, what Welwood has named basic aliveness. This is not a level that is normally experienced unless we quieten down some of the other levels of experience. It is nevertheless ever present as an aspect of the innate nature of the mind in relation to the vitality of our life.

In the tantric tradition this vitality has a particular significance because it is seen as a facet of our being that underlies every aspect of the mind. In Tibetan this is called *lung*, or energy winds; in Sanskrit it is *prana;* in Chinese it is called *chi*. In chapter 13, I will explore this phenomenon in more detail.

Differentiating the levels of this map requires that we learn to listen to our inner life and notice more clearly what is going on. Only when we do this can we start to apply more subtle language to our experience more subtly. For some this is very easy; for others it has to be learned. As a man growing up in a world where men tended not to be emotionally literate, this learning has been a very necessary process. In my family there was little or no expression of feelings, and our emotions were usually more repressed—except in my father, who tended to have rages. This did not give me a particularly good ground for listening to what I felt and then being able to name those feelings. Even so, I was more aware of my feelings than I was able to acknowledge in growing up, and I found it something of a relief when I realized that my feelings were acceptable and could be communicated.

As we delve into the layers of this feeling world, what becomes apparent is that we are in relationship to the environment on all of them. We notice this most obviously with our senses, but there are subtler, less obvious levels. If I sit in a room full of people, I may not at first recognize that I am picking up something that is going on for another person in the room. This may be happening on a felt-sense level, but I have not yet recognized it. I may then start to experience some stronger feeling about someone and suddenly become aware of what is happening. This happens to us all the time, but we may not be listening on that level. Equally, we may not notice the emergence of the storm clouds of stronger feelings as they become an emotional reaction until we are taken over by them. This may have begun, as I suggested in the beginning of this chapter, as a small wisp of felt sense that grew into something very powerful.

Finding the language of our feeling life is, of course, central to the psychotherapy world. It is this emphasis on the exploration of feelings that has led some Buddhist practitioners and teachers to consider therapy to be somewhat indulgent. The occasional dismissal of the value of our feeling life by some Buddhist teachers is something that I feel needs to be challenged. There is the danger of making our feeling life merely another level of delusion that has to be abandoned because we take too much notice of it. This may also be where our East-West cultural differences will reflect different views of the application of Buddhist teachings. Western meditators who manage to bypass or divorce their meditation from their feeling life do so at great risk to the resolution of their emotional problems. It is then too easy to think that we have developed deep meditation experience and then to discover that we have not addressed our emotional problems at all.

I was at one time in conversation with a man who had been through a three-year meditation retreat during which a huge amount of pain and trauma emerged. Regrettably, his Tibetan teachers seemed to find it hard to comprehend what he was experiencing; it was not part of their education, and therefore they did not really know how to support him through it. On finishing his retreat, he found the resources of Western psychologists and psychotherapists who were able to shed some light on what was emerging and how to be with it. This man was an interesting example of someone who clearly had some significant meditation experiences but still needed to balance these with a greater resolution to the emotional life that had been evoked in his practice. Increasingly, I am contacted by people who have had a similar experience, finding that even though they are experienced Buddhist practitioners, their practice has led them to the realization that they need to include greater psychological awareness of the significance of emotional life.

The avoidance or our feeling life overlooks the reality that it is this deepening experience of feeling that is also at the heart of our awakening. Subtler levels of mind experienced in meditation are always accompanied by ever-subtler levels of feeling. Feeling does not just cease as we go deeper; it is an ever-present aspect of the mind. That means that it is through this domain of emotion and the subtle undercurrents of feeling that we deepen, not by avoiding, suppressing, or denying it. In order to make this journey, however, we need to look at the way in which emotional and feeling processes affect our mind and its view of reality.

4

delusions
and emotions

WHAT BECOMES VERY CLEAR through Buddhist
teachings is that the suffering and problems we have
in life are not caused by external circumstances but by the
mind that reacts to them. The mind dominated by delusions
or emotional afflictions is considered in Buddhism to be
the cause of most of the suffering and problems that arise
in our life and more generally in the world at large. We can
certainly see the truth in this view when we look at the way
fear, hatred, and greed seem to be at the root of many if not
most of the problems that exist in the world, from wars to
the banking crisis. From this viewpoint we can also see that
if we had a greater awareness of the emotions that drive us,
both individually and collectively, our world would be very

different. There is no doubt that when the mind is dominated by destructive emotions, it is essentially out of control
and gives rise to so many problems. From this perspective the
aim of Buddhist practice is to tame the mind so that these
emotional afflictions do not arise. One aspect of this is recognizing how we react to the raw experiences of pleasant and
unpleasant feeling. The important question that arises is,
therefore, how do we "tame the mind" in a way that is both
skillful and healthy and does not simply repress emotions?
We also need to begin to discern the difference between our
emotional life that is a natural expression of who we are and
that which becomes destructive and bound by delusion.

The term *delusion* is an interesting one and is usually
the translation of the term *klesha* in Sanskrit or *nyonmong* in
Tibetan. At some times this term *nyonmong* is translated as
"delusion" and at others as "emotional affliction," two expressions that are very different in their implications. It is
important to consider that the term *nyonmong* is not a direct
equivalent of the word *emotion,* even though it may have an
emotional component; indeed, there would seem to be no
equivalent term in either Tibetan or Sanskrit. Delusion is
therefore not the same as emotion but is a way of seeing the
world that is intimately associated with our emotional life.
When we look at our actual experience of the arising of emotions and many of the subtler feelings, we can begin to see
that this emotional or felt tone is very often accompanied by
a particular coloring of reality. When we experience a strong
feeling/emotion like fear, we can see this very clearly. Fear
brings with it a range of emotional reactions that are felt
strongly in the body. There can be a quickening of the pulse,

a tightening of the abdomen, sweating, and rushing energy throughout the body. What we may not recognize is that our fear can also color our experience. What this means is that the way we are seeing the things we fear can be distorted by our projections. If it is a person we fear, for example, we may color that person with all manner of projections that make us believe that person is a threat even if he or she may not be.

In the Tibetan world there is a familiar example of this experience that has become something of a cliché. If we saw a coiled, shadowy appearance at the side of the path when walking along in the dark, we might immediately experience a feeling of shock and fear because it looks like a snake. When we investigate more closely, we recognize that it is actually a coiled rope or a garden hose. The combination of the external appearance and the emotional response creates what might be seen as an illusion. If we were to consider this in different circumstances, we would recognize that when strong emotions arise, they are nearly always accompanied by a projected view of the world that is usually considered to be a distortion of what actually exists. Strong emotions almost always, therefore, color the world and our reality whether we are considering positive or negative ones. It is the combination of these two characteristics of emotion and distorted projection that the Tibetans would describe to be a delusion or emotional affliction.

There is, however, an important distinction that is not always apparent in the way some Buddhists speak about delusions and emotional afflictions. We need to distinguish between emotions and destructive emotional afflictions. This distinction is made clear by the Dalai Lama when he says we

need to "distinguish between two sub-categories: those emotional states that are destructive in themselves such as greed,
hatred, or malice; and those states such as attachment, anger,
or fear, which only become destructive when their intensity is
disproportionate to the situation in which they arise."[1] In this
comment the Dalai Lama is reinforcing an understanding in
Western psychology that emotional states are not inherently
destructive and can be an important response to particular
contexts. Where they become problematic is when their intensity is so great that they become destructive both to oneself
and to others because they seriously disturb the mind.

Perhaps the example of fear is a useful one. It is natural
and necessary to experience fear if, for example, someone
were threatening us with a knife or if we were standing close
to the edge of a dangerous highway with traffic moving past at
great speed. This fear does not carry projected delusion. It is
the reality of danger. However, when I am walking down the
street and see a stranger across the road whom I fear because
of the color of his skin, this fear carries with it all manner of
potential prejudices that distort my view of someone who is
probably not a threat. This fear carries with it a delusion.

In Buddhism six primary delusions are recognized, namely:
attachment, aversion, pride, envy, doubt, and ignorance.
Among these, perhaps the two most important are attachment and aversion, where attachment is seen as the response
to pleasant feelings and aversion the response to unpleasant
ones. These delusions have associated clusters of emotional
states, so that attachment can be associated with greed, lust,
desire, yearning, hunger, dissatisfaction, and a range of other
feelings. Here the delusional aspect is that the mind exag-

gerates and distorts the value of something and then seeks to have contact with it.

Aversion as a delusion is often associated with emotions of hatred, anger, repulsion, malice, resentment, and even jealousy. When these feelings are constellated is that they lead us to exaggerate the negative attributes of an object, onto which we then project and feel aversion toward. Each of the other delusions can have associated emotional states as well, so pride can bring arrogance, conceit, prejudice, and grandiosity; envy can bring jealousy, dissatisfaction, desire, and even anger; doubt can bring lack of confidence, inadequacy, fear, and uncertainty. Ignorance is a state of mind that is associated with feelings of indifference, boredom, disinterest, or even a kind of cut-off dissociation that does not wish to engage with an object or make real contact. This level of ignorance does not recognize the nature of what is out there as being of any value or significance.

What we see in this view is that the delusion is based on projection and then has an accompanying emotional expression. We can look at this traditional distinction of the primary delusions, or we could consider our emotional life in a more psychological sense.

Working as a psychotherapist, something that becomes very apparent to me is that we are often taken over by emotional states arising from the unconscious that are triggered by an external event. This is a view shared, of course, by Buddhist thinking, although there is no notion of the unconscious in Buddhism. This can mean that some aspect of our unconscious life is invoked and will often bring with it a cluster of emotions. For example, if someone pushes our buttons, we may find ourselves suddenly taken over by a childlike part of ourselves that has feelings of hurt, pain, rage, need, abandonment, and so on. When these strong emotions arise, they will inevitably flavor the whole of our experience by projections that are related to that child part of ourselves. We may see the person or situation as though it were a very powerful echo of some childhood experience and yet be unconscious of the fact. Some aspect of our past history is awakened and projected into the present-day experience. We believe what we are seeing as a true reality, not realizing it is a projection. This is the kind of experience many people have who have had difficult experiences earlier in life. Relationships can then become charged with past history.

At such times it can become painfully clear that we are actually caught in what might be described as a delusion, a projection, but we may also be completely unable to see it. We may find we are absolutely convinced by what we see. The arising of strong emotions of what we might call the inner child brings with it a host of projections that color the world in a particular way. Perhaps one problem with the use of the term *delusion* is that it can feel somewhat judgmental rather than simply indicating that what our mind and unconscious do is project. (One reason that the term *delusion* is problematic is that it has often been used in the case of those with severe psychiatric disorders.) In the therapeutic context, however, the process of projection is actually very significant because it enables a more conscious relationship for both client and therapist. Sometimes, for example, a client may say that she does not feel safe or that she feels abandoned and lost in a very painful world if I go away. While these feelings are triggered by the present, they have been drawn out of the client's past. This leads to very young emotions coming through that may completely see me as a terrible abandoning parent who is untrustworthy and who doesn't really care. When this kind of projection occurs, a client may be convinced of this reality and only gradually begin to see that, in fact, this is not the case in the present, that I do care and that she is not being abandoned. To describe this process as merely delusion is to miss the significance of its origins and the understanding that can emerge from it.

One of the most common experiences of reality being colored by our emotional life is when we experience depression. The emotional tone of depression may be a flat deadness; it can be extremely painful and despairing; it can be full of anger and self-reproach. Whatever we experience on a feeling level will also bring with it a powerful projection into the world. We can project that our life is pointless and lacks any value, that it is going nowhere and no one cares about us, and so on. The world becomes gray and drab, devoid of color and vitality. We are caught in an illusion that combines a strong emotional tone with a powerful disturbing projection. The combination of these two can be extremely difficult to bear, and thus our conceptual mind will take great delight in creating ever more stories about how bad things are.

This leads us to recognize that there is a third factor at work in this process, namely, the conceptual mind. It is interesting that in his translation of Shantideva's *Guide to the Bodhisattva's Way of Life,* Stephen Batchelor chose to render the term usually translated as *emotional afflictions* as *disturbing conceptions.* If we take the idea of disturbing conception, it brings out the third factor in our emotional life: that our emotions and delusions are almost always accompanied by a host of conceptions about our experience. Compulsively, our mind becomes full of thoughts, worries, and beliefs about what we are experiencing, which stimulate feelings even more. Take, for example, the experience of doubt. With doubt there can be a strong anxious emotional tone as well as all kinds of illusions about what we doubt. Perhaps most of all, our mind becomes caught in the "disturbing conceptions" about being inadequate or incapable. These thoughts can be terribly debilitating, as they undermine our confidence and capacity. Sometimes it is the conceptual disturbance that has the most power over us as we struggle to deal with the inner voices that criticize and abuse us or continually remind us of our fears and anxieties.

As we become more familiar with these three dimensions of our emotional process, we will also recognize that at their core is a charged and wounded sense of self. Whenever these emotional reactions arise, they will constellate around a sense of self that has a particular flavor—usually painful and negative, but not always. At the heart of these manifestations of our emotional experience is the feeling of "me" that arises vividly. This is the central sense of what is known in Tibetan as *dagdzin*, or ego grasping. From a Buddhist point of view, it is this ego-grasping tendency that holds the sense of self—albeit often an emotionally wounded one—as solid and permanent. It is this sense of self that, through meditation, is seen to be empty of solid, inherent existence.

Finally, when we bring together a more complete psychological picture of this emotional patterning, we then need to include the fact that from this emotional/delusional place we react to our experience in a way that either contracts into and grasps at our experience or pushes it away and rejects it. These two reactive habits around our experiences are instinctual and bring us to respond to the environment around us through our behavior. If we placed these dimensions of emotional life in a map, it could look something like figure 2 (see page 36).

Beginning to deal with this emotional life is a challenge for all of us and is one of the factors that often lead us to explore something like Buddhism. Within Buddhism we then find a variety of approaches, which can have their own value in different circumstances. On one level we may find that the capacity to be more aware of this process in ourselves is relatively straightforward. The more we watch and get to know our emotional reactions, the more we may be able to have some control over them. We may recognize situations where we are becoming caught up in some kind of emotional reaction that is unhelpful and counter the process. Meditation and the practice of mindfulness can be extremely helpful, as they enable us to cultivate a greater capacity to watch what is arising in our mind. We should not think, however, that meditation alone is going to be the answer to all of our emotional problems. Meditation can be a valuable aid to developing a greater awareness and insight into our emotional life, helping us to see more clearly the projections of our mind upon our reality when emotions arise. For some of us, however, the strength of our emotional problems and their complexity can suggest that we may also have to do some kind of therapeutic work to resolve them. From my experience as both a meditator and a psychotherapist, I have seen that some of our emotional wounds need more than meditation practices to resolve them. Unless

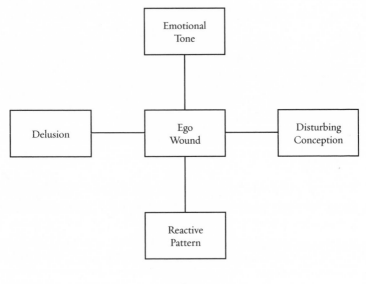

FIG. 2.

we are helped to look more deeply into our wounding, we may not be able to get to it. Meditation does not necessarily do this, and many people have come to me saying that they have been practicing for many years and yet still have not addressed some core issues.

I said at the beginning of this chapter that the inclusion of emotion as an aspect of *nyonmong,* or delusion, may give the impression that emotion is therefore bad and destructive or to be abandoned or tamed, and that when we overcome our emotional life, we will have achieved some sort of liberation. This may be the impression one gets where there is great emphasis on delusion and so-called destructive emotions. But as the Dalai Lama says, "The important point to bear in mind is that these feelings are not destructive in themselves;

they become destructive only when their intensity is out of proportion to the situation, or when they arise in situations that do not call for them."[2]

Many of our emotions have deep instinctual and psychological roots that should not automatically be assumed to be delusions. Fear, for example, is an extremely important capacity that alerts us to danger and can then enable us to act. Equally sadness and grief are very natural expressions of loss and need to be allowed to pass through; they are not just attachment. Anger can even have an important place in our life as the underlying energy that asserts a clear boundary, for example, when it is needed to protect ourselves or our family. Desire is a natural expression of our movement toward something that is significant to us. Our emotions, as the Latin origins of the word imply, move us into action; they become problematic only when we are dominated by their strength and allow them to rule us in unhealthy ways. They become a basis for suffering when we contract into them, solidify our experience, and become reactive. Emotions become particularly problematic when they are contaminated by a strong distortion in the way we perceive something. This distortion is the delusion that can turn ordinary emotions into destructive emotions, which then increase in intensity.

Perhaps as Buddhist views and Western psychological understanding come together, we can begin to find a more-developed understanding of our emotional life—one that recognizes that emotions per se are not the same as delusions and are not always destructive but actually have a place in our life. We can also begin to see that there is a spectrum of experience of emotions that can begin as a relatively natural felt response to certain circumstances but can lead to more-intense, distorted, and destructive levels. How well we live with our emotional life is then going to depend upon the degree to which we are able to be aware of what is happening within.

When we look more deeply into emotional life, we will see that it does, indeed, color our view of reality. It does sometimes lead to delusions that project onto and distort our experience of reality. It also stimulates a huge amount of discursive conceptual chatter that can be extremely disturbing. However, as we become more familiar with the different ingredients of our emotional life, what will become very obvious is the complexity of our emotional patterning and its influence over us. It is this complexity that leads many of us either to go into therapy or to embark upon some kind of meditation practice, or both.

If we can be more observant of our emotional processes and see them more clearly, we will begin to have choices around our response to them. Freeing ourselves from the unconscious dominance of emotions requires that we be able to engage them with greater awareness. To avoid the movement of our emotional life toward what might be seen as destructive, we also need to be able to recognize and clear the delusional aspect of projection that turns relatively normal emotional states into their more-destructive nature. If we are able to witness them without losing ourselves in them and becoming taken over by them, we then begin to disidentify and separate from them, to use a common psychological term. When we are able to look into the nature of our emotional life with awareness, we can also more readily separate out what is beneficial from what is potentially unhealthy or even destructive. Disidentification is helped by the process of psychotherapy; it can also be helped by an increased capacity for mindfulness developed in meditation. Unless we can begin to disidentify, however, we cannot move forward and transform the emotions. I will go into this in more depth in later chapters.

AWARENESS CHOICE TRUST

moods

THERE IS ONE OTHER AREA of feeling life that I think is worthy of reflection, and that relates to moods. We could see moods as simply a more diffuse area of emotion that has less specific definition, but there is more to it than that. As a young man in my twenties, I became acutely aware that I could easily become trapped in moods. I am not alone in this, and for anyone in relationship with a person who goes into moods, it is an extremely difficult thing to deal with or live with. Both men and women can experience moods, and the common element is that it is often very difficult for the person caught in a mood to get out of it. It is also very hard for someone in a mood to be aware of or witness what is going on.

From a Jungian point of view, what is interesting about the
mood is that it bears a particular relationship to the unconscious. I have, in the previous chapter, described how we can
lose ourselves in strong emotions as though we were drowning. This happens in a more insidious way with moods, which
are not always so obviously dominated by a particularly strong
emotion. Even so, in moods we are being drawn into the unconscious in a way that is very intractable. Although in Buddhist thinking there is no concept of the unconscious, Jung's
view is very useful in clarifying certain psychological experiences. His view of the unconscious as a dimension of the mind
or psyche that is below the level of conscious awareness has
given us an understanding that many things that go on within
us are "beneath" our awareness; they are unconscious. Jung's
view of the unconscious is that it is like a realm of the psyche,
a container that holds aspects of our emotional life. The contents of the unconscious may emerge and affect us as though
they had some kind of autonomy when activated by our experiences. They can have a life of their own outside of the control of our conscious mind.

When we consider the idea of the unconscious, we find that
there is another way that it affects us. We can become drawn
into the unconscious as though drawn beneath the surface of
water. In effect, when strong emotional processes are activated that have a dominating power over us, we have become
pulled into the unconscious. Our conscious mind struggles to
retain awareness while we are possessed by our inner psychological life. This can be very disturbing and overwhelming.
From a Buddhist viewpoint, we could say that most of us are
largely unconscious most of the time because we lack a sharp

quality of present awareness. In the case of moods, however, the power of the unconscious has a subtly different effect in that it is as though we were in a kind of swoon that we cannot easily come out of. *Moods & passive aggression* –

With moods, this pull into the unconscious is going on in a way that is often less obviously emotionally charged and yet will often contain some strong dispositions usually barely known by the person in the mood. This is because there is no witness of the experience—effectively, we *are* it. Anyone outside of it and receiving the impact of someone's mood, however, can be aware of certain characteristic feelings about the mood. Moods have an atmosphere that may hold a lot of what is called passive aggression. This means that the aggressive tendency has gone underground and is being expressed as a kind of mood of resistance. A mood may contain a kind of punishing element where, again subtly, the person in the mood is giving off a desire to hurt or punish another person. There can also be a level of stubbornness that is very powerful and determined in a negative, inverted way—an intractability that may be felt by an outside recipient. One other aspect of the mood can be a level of victim-like self-pity or self-berating that goes on within the atmosphere of the mood. Moods will often have a level of spiky irritability about them that turns into anger very quickly.

Moods have an atmosphere that is picked up by others and is often directed at others for a particular effect. Moods may contain some element of subtle anger or blame that is very unconscious and has its origins in childhood. For this reason it can be very uncomfortable to be around someone in a mood. Anyone who gets these moods and is willing to be honest about the nature of them will be aware that there is something very childlike or adolescent about them. There is also something that can seem very self-indulgent and stubborn about them. The most natural response from anyone outside is to try to get the person to snap out of it, but this is virtually impossible for the person in the mood because when in this state, we are effectively enthralled by the unconscious. It is as though the unconscious had imprisoned us in its power, and there is, therefore, little or no conscious volition or conscious capacity to see objectively what is happening and climb out.

There is a scene in the *Lord of the Rings* trilogy that is a vivid metaphor for how some moods can affect us. Frodo, Sam, and Gollum are crossing a marsh, and beneath the surface of the water they can see the souls of the dead with blank, staring expressions. Frodo's mood is very close to a state of dreamy despair, and he gazes into the water and is sucked in to where he would have drowned if Gollum had not grabbed him and pulled him out. This is a vivid and graphic metaphor for the power of moods over our conscious awareness when we are unable to resist the tendency to sink into the depths of the unconscious.

One particular example of this power of the unconscious to pull us into a mood is found in men who are still psychologically dominated by their mother—not necessarily their actual mother any longer but an internalized presence of the mother. A man dominated in this way can become trapped in a mood that is very dark and self-berating but that is often triggered by feeling hurt or dominated by a partner. Women experiencing this in their male partners will sense a very childlike, closed, and unreachable state that is nevertheless giving off a mixture of punishing or needy feelings that often relate to the mother. From Jung's perspective, this is where men have become overwhelmed by the dominance of the unconscious, bringing with it all the emotional moods of a child in reaction to the mother. Only by gradually waking up to the nature of this tendency can a man find the capacity not to sink into this kind of mood. It almost requires an act of will to do so, which comes with a kind of growing up.

Jung also described what he called the anima mood, where we can be overwhelmed, entranced, or beguiled by the powerful presence of the psyche's capacity to fill us with images and fantasy.[1] This can create a kind of absent dreaminess that is caused by being absorbed in another world. This can happen for both men and women when we are lost in the unconscious, perhaps as a way of avoiding outside reality. The Pre-Raphaelite artists were very fond of painting this kind of mood in the expression of some of their heroines, who would be depicted gazing dreamily into space as though they were not present but were somewhere far away. The anima mood may mean we become lost in a world that is full of semiconscious fantasy. This fantasy may be pleasant in nature, but it can equally be dark and brooding. Some may become lost in a world of pain and torment, as in the case of someone who is shut away in some kind of trauma and caught in a deep inner hell. Again, when I have worked in the therapeutic setting with people in this place, it can feel extremely uncomfortable for me as the therapist because the impact of this inner world is hard to bear.

Moods are an interesting dimension of our feeling life because they are not felt very consciously. Rather, they are sunk into as though we were absorbed into the unconscious, which from a Jungian point of view is exactly what has happened. In my own experience of wrestling with this tendency in my twenties, I became very aware that it took time for a mood to wear off and that it was often best to be left alone during this time. Any attempt from a partner or friend to get me out of it would usually drive me deeper in and out of reach. It could also bring out a depth of anger and hopelessness that was unbearable. With time I could see that by an act of almost conscious determination I could resist the temptation to be sucked into the water and drown. I could more readily lift myself out, and the habit began to decline. We can do this, however, only when we are willing to acknowledge the effect the mood has on us and are willing to wake up and resist the unconscious pull.

Possibly the most problematic aspect of moods is that they are ripe ground from which strong emotions can emerge. In Buddhism it is often said that anger, particularly, arises from an unhappy mind. This is certainly true of the unhappiness that is present with moods. It does not always take much for the person in a mood to be provoked into strong emotional reactions, as though the emotions were just waiting for a reason to come out. Sometimes moods can lift after an emotional outbreak, but it can also be that the person will remain irritable and negative for long periods.

While moods may not fall into the traditional category of feelings and emotions, they are nevertheless something that some of us have to face. Moods are subtly charged with feeling that is often diffuse, which others may experience as an uncomfortable atmosphere. The challenge with moods is to become awake to free our mind from the unconscious pull they create. While moods may not be as obviously destructive as strong emotions, they can nevertheless be painful and problematic, especially to those who have to endure their presence in someone they are close to. Often intimate relationships suffer serious problems when one or the other partner has a tendency to sink into moods. It then requires some determination for the moody person to change and lift out of the unconscious enthrallment that moods bring.

Moods, like other emotional states, are most effectively countered by waking up and becoming aware within them. The process of meditation and mindfulness may help in this, as it may strengthen the capacity for conscious awareness. Then we can begin to lift ourselves out of the water and not drown. This may require a relatively determined willingness to emerge rather than just allow a sliding down into the unconscious.

6

the discernment
of feeling

B EFORE I START TO EXPLORE the way in which we may
begin to work with the realm of feeling, I would like to
describe another way in which feeling can be understood.
This view is one that was developed by C. G. Jung as a way
of understanding what he called the feeling function, and I
would like to make some comparisons with the feeling aggregate that is considered in Buddhism.[1] Jung, in the development of his extraordinary view of the psyche, proposed a map
that has been adapted by later psychologists. He saw that we
know the world through what he described as the four functions: thinking, feeling, intuition, and sensation.[2] A varia-
tion of these may be familiar to some readers through the
Meyers-Briggs type indicator, which was derived from Jung's

work. What Jung believed was that we each tend to know the world through one of these functions in particular, what he called the dominant function. The dominance of one makes the other three less developed, and one in particular becomes what he called the recessive function. Jung paired these functions as opposites such that thinking and feeling formed one pair of opposites and intuition and sensation the other. This can be mapped as below.

Although the thinking function has been placed at the top, we should not consider that therefore it is somehow more important. To describe these functions briefly: someone who is predominantly thinking in her or his orientation will see the world through the vehicle of reason and the intellect, creating

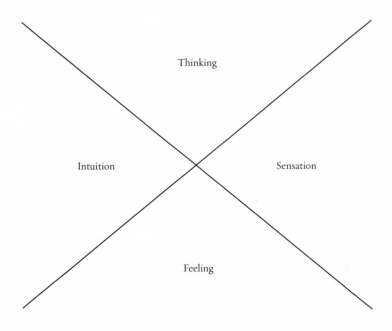

FIG. 3.

conceptual views and maps that order and shape experience. The intuitive person will see the world through the vehicle of the unconscious and will be particularly concerned with meaning and symbolic language in making sense of what he or she experiences and what it represents. This kind of person may be very imaginative, letting intuition color his or her creativity and sense of meaning. The sensation-function person tends to see the world through its factual information. If things can be measured and organized, then they will make sense. The sensate might say "Prove it to me and I will believe it."

Finally, we come to the feeling function, which for the sake of this current exploration I wish to go into in more detail. The feeling function is a way in which we assess the world by how things feel. Feeling in this respect is less a kind of affect and more a means of gauging or assessing how something is. There is, in feeling, a quality of discernment that knows very deeply that something does or does not feel right. To a feeling-function person, the question "How do you feel about this?" is perhaps the most relevant question of all. Jung saw the feeling function as a discriminating capacity that enables us to evaluate and separate out what we feel is acceptable and what is not. It is this capacity that he felt was of great significance as the basis for the principle of ethics. He saw ethical awareness as not based in reason but deeply rooted in feeling.

Although I wish to look at a Jungian perspective here, it is perhaps useful to compare this with the feeling aggregate that is found in Buddhism. In making this comparison, however, I am not saying these are merely different views of the same thing. As we will see, they are a different order of experience. In Buddhist thinking, as I have suggested earlier, one aspect of our nature is what is known as the aggregate (Skt., *skandha*) of feeling. This aggregate is seen as an ever-present mental factor that arises in every experience as a discernment of pleasant, unpleasant, or neutral feeling. This discernment is seen as the basis from which we then enter into the range of reactions and judgments we place upon our experiences. "Feeling," the usual translation of the Tibetan *tsorwa,* is perhaps more akin to our idea of sensation and is a natural and immediate evaluation of what we experience through the senses, which causes us to be attracted to some things and feel aversion to others. From a Buddhist point of view, this process is helpful, and one could say necessary, as it enables us to gauge what is safe or unsafe or what is helpful or not, but it is also seen as a problem because it gives rise to what are known as the three poisons of desire, aversion, and ignorance. While in the West we may give much attention to feeling, from a traditional Buddhist viewpoint, feeling is fickle, unreliable, and unstable and has little inherent value. It is for this reason that we are often taught by Eastern Buddhist teachers not to be too involved in our feelings because they make us unstable and changeable. If we are less controlled by our feelings, they believe, we will then find peace and happiness. A primary intention of meditation within the Theravada traditions in particular is to develop the capacity to watch and observe the natural arising of feeling so as to become liberated from the tendency to react. Finding a level of detached disidentification from feeling enables us to live with greater awareness of the ways in which feeling drives our life.

This view of feeling is very important to understand but also has a somewhat negative implication that still suggests that feeling is not of much value. We could say that *tsorwa* is the simplest level of feeling/sensation in its raw and primary state. It is a capacity of discernment that evaluates our experience in a very direct and immediate and nonconceptual way. From a psychological view we could also say that this aspect of feeling has some resonance with our early childhood experience of feeling/sensation experienced in the body before it became more differentiated as a psychological aspect of our nature. Learning to be mindful of this basic arising of feeling is central to many Buddhist practices, as it enables us to be less caught in our reactions. In a more positive sense, this aggregate provides a means of evaluating and responding to our experiences. The feeling aggregate gives us a very immediate piece of sensory information that we learn to discern and evaluate in a much more subtle psychological way than just a pleasure/pain paradigm. Jung's view of the feeling function is in this respect a much more differentiated and developed psychological aspect of feeling, which he recognized has an extremely valuable and necessary place in our life. Perhaps what these two dimensions of feeling have in common is that each functions like a thermometer, one providing a raw and immediate evaluation, the other a more psychologically complex one. Without them we would have many difficulties, we would have no means of discerning what is acceptable and what is not, what is comfortable and what is not, and—perhaps more instinctually—what is safe and what is not.

In the map of Jung's four functions, we see that he placed them in relation to what he saw as their natural opposites. This pairing of opposite functions has many implications in how we experience our life. It means that someone who is predominantly a thinking-function person will have what Jung called an inferior or less-developed feeling function and vice versa. If someone is an intuitive, the person will have an inferior sensation function, and a sensation-function person will have an inferior intuitive function. By *inferior,* he implied that this side of our nature is not very conscious: it will be a challenge to us, and in that area we will often feel a bit inadequate. The dominant function, on the other hand, is immediate and easy. It is a mode of understanding that we automatically use even though we may not recognize that until it is pointed out to us. Jung's theory of the four functions is very useful in doing exactly that: it can show us what our tendency is.

I have often found a useful way of discerning the difference in these functions by considering the way a person might reflect upon the moon through each of these functions. The thinking-function person will be interested in the nature of the moon as a planet in orbit around the earth and how it was created through the collision of planets. The sensation-function person may be more inclined toward the appearance of the moon as a white disk in the dark sky with curious shades on it, wondering how large it is and how far it is from the earth. The intuitive looks at the moon and has a sense of mystery, considering its meaning and the manifestations of the goddess of the moon and the archetypal qualities in her cycle. The feeling-function person will bathe in the wonderful feeling of the night, with the still, clear radiance of the bright and beautiful moon, and be filled with a sense of how good it feels to be there.

Feeling is obviously far more subjective than either thinking or sensation and requires a much more inward gaze to listen to what we are actually feeling. Through our feeling sense we have the capacity to assess whether the world is trust-worthy or false, whether it is caring or not, whether it is just or not. Those with a strong feeling function will often have an acute sense of injustice.

Jung once wrote that it is the feeling function that pro-vides the basis for a sense of morality that is not governed by outer prescriptions but, rather, by a felt inner discern-ment. In this he shared a view similar to that of the eminent eighteenth-century Scottish philosopher David Hume, who considered that it was our emotional nature that determined the ethical basis of our life, not reason itself. Hume asserted that humankind had the capacity for an ethical basis to our nature based upon feeling that was not dependent on God. Jung considered that without a relationship to feeling we would act in ways that were potentially harmful to others because we would have no empathic gauge to tell us that what we were doing was not acceptable. He gave the example of the surgeons who performed dreadful operations without anesthetic upon people in the German concentration camps during the Second World War. If these people, he said, had had a genuine relationship to their feeling function, they would not have been able to commit such atrocities. He be-lieved that they must have deeply buried this capacity.

A more recent example of this feeling ethic arose when the UK government declared that it was contemplating allowing the cultivation of genetically modified crops. There was an instant response from thousands of people who simply felt it was not acceptable.

There are those for whom feeling is a deep and very pri-vate aspect of life, and yet it is a constant undercurrent that is there to give a kind of guidance. When this is the case, our feeling function may require time to allow us to "feel into" our response. For me it is this slower working of the feeling function that often requires me to respond to someone's question with the comment "Give me a while and I will get back to you." I need time to feel whether to say yes or no based not upon reason and logic but upon how I feel about it. My feeling function is a clear gauge of whether situations seem acceptable or not; one might call it a gut feeling. If I suspect someone is not clear or honest or has some underlying agenda, then my feeling function senses it.

With the feeling function we may also need time to detect feelings that are still caught in some reactive process that clouds our discernment. This is often where people say that when they listen to their feelings, all they get is a confused sense of emotional conflict between differing emotions such as fear, expectation, doubt, and anxiety. When we can tune in to another level of clear discernment, we begin to get a truer sense of what we feel about something.

For someone with an acute feeling function, it can be difficult to give a reason for what is felt. It may be equally difficult to express the feeling verbally so that those without this feeling reference can understand or recognize the validity of the feeling. This is often where the thinking-function person and the feeling-function person get into deep trouble in their communication. The feeling-function person may be saying that something simply doesn't feel right, but the thinker is wanting some clear-cut reasons for it. This doesn't work for the feeler; indeed, there is often no way to justify the feeling, nor is there the need to do so. People who have a good feeling function are often very clear, especially around ethical issues. The feeling-function person will very quickly sniff out something that is not ethical and in this respect is an invaluable resource in our world.

If we are predominantly a thinking-function person—or, indeed, one of the other two functions—then our feeling function may be relatively less developed or less conscious. This can lead the thinker, in particular, to feel out of depth in the feeling world and therefore somewhat defensive about it. This implies not that a thinking-function person cannot develop the feeling function but that it requires some further psychological work. Thinking-function people are often very attracted to relationship with those who have a strong feeling function. This is because there is a tendency to project out into the world what we are unconscious of and then be attracted by it because of its difference. Unfortunately, in relationships where thinking and feeling people do get together, this combination can lead to huge misunderstandings as they struggle to communicate across the psychological divide. They will view the same situations in such differing ways and seldom agree on what they see. It is only in the course of gradually opening to and respecting the other position that some sense of mutual understanding comes about.

I introduce this aspect of feeling because if we understand the relevance of the function of feeling, we will see that it is one of the most important psychological touchstones we have. We learn to differentiate among an emotional reaction, a feeling-function response, and the feeling-aggregate response. They are all potentially present within certain situations and we do not recognize the different processes

going on. When we listen to the discerning side of our feeling nature, it will give a deep knowing that is more heartfelt
than our intellect's. But experiencing this capacity requires
us to quieten our mind so that we can listen to its felt insight. So often we are unfamiliar with listening to our inner
truth around how we feel about something. It is then noticeable that when the question is asked, "How do you feel about
something?" we cannot really answer. This absence of a feeling response suggests that we really need to stop, slow down,
and begin to listen to ourselves on this level. Only then will
we be able to have a sense of what is okay for us and what
is not. If we cannot do this, we may find, as many do, that
sometime down the road we suddenly begin to realize that we
are doing something that we really did not want to do. This
can lead to all manner of resentments, feeling that we are vic-
tims of what is happening because we did not choose it. If we
learn to listen to this quieter voice of feeling, we will know
what is important and be able to make choices based upon
some sense of knowing what is true for us. Lama Yeshe would
often say "Trust your inner wisdom," and in many ways it is
this feeling function that he is referring to.

People with a developed feeling function will generally be
more at home with the world of feelings and emotions. We all
have this capacity, but for some it is more readily developed
than for others. Once we are able to live with our feeling life
in a more discerning way, then our feeling function can be a
crucial guide in life.

reflection
or presence

W HEN I FIRST BECAME involved in the Tibetan tradition, the approach I was given for dealing with
emotions was in many ways cognitive in nature. It was oriented to an idea that if we create a cognitive reassessment
of our emotional life, it will change. The teachings of mind
training, or *lojong,* as it is called, are designed to reevaluate
what we are going through so that we eventually think about
experiences we are going through differently and therefore
hopefully feel differently also. We were taught to reflect
upon the positive qualities that would act as an antidote to
negative emotional states. In many ways this has parallels
with the modern approach of what is known as cognitive
therapy, where we are asked to reframe our view of what we

are going through, thereby changing the way we feel about them. A typical example of this would be turning what we consider to be a problem into a challenge.

When we reflect upon our experience, it can give us an alternative way to see things, and it will enable us to understand ourselves better. We can unearth experiences from the past that help us to make sense of our life and our emotional reactions and patterning. While this kind of therapeutic reflection on the personal story is not usually considered within Buddhist psychology because attention tends to focus more in the present, it is nevertheless a valuable exploration. When we apply the kind of principles contained within the *lojong* teachings, we are being asked to reconsider the basis of what we feel. For example, if I have strong angry or irritated feelings toward someone I know, the *lojong* principle would be along the lines of seeing that person as a great asset because he teaches me the most about myself. We try to consider that that person has his own problems, which is why he is the way he is. If we feel unhappy about something that has gone wrong, we try to think that this is impermanent and we are only suffering because of our attachment to self. In his *Guide to the Bodhisattva's Way of Life*, Shantideva asks why we should be angry at the stick that someone hits us with when it is controlled by the person holding it?[1] In the same way, why should I be angry at the person who harms me, when he is also driven by his emotional afflictions?

Lojong and the more-reflective, cognitive ways of dealing with our emotional life can help us in small ways to live with greater tolerance and understanding of the kinds of problems that arise in our life. We may, through greater understanding, have more control over how we react to situations that cause us concern. Having spent many of my early years as a Buddhist reflecting in this way on the things that affect my life, I have had a very direct sense of its value. The teachings and meditations of what is known as the Lam Rim, or graduated path, offer a very clear basis for reflecting upon our life and changing the way we respond to life situations.

Within the world of psychotherapy, the process of reflection has been extremely important in giving us a way to evaluate and describe our feelings and emotions by telling their story. This can lead us to understand the roots of our feelings more fully and look at some of our beliefs and attitudes found within them. It will also give us a chance to consider the things that have led us to react to the world in a particular way. We begin to delve into the history of our emotional life and the kind of influences and wounds that may have occurred, particularly in early childhood. In psychotherapy this has been the basis of what is sometimes called talk therapy, where perhaps for the first time a person has the chance to speak about her or his experiences in a secure, nonjudgmental, and compassionate context. For many people there can be huge relief in having someone to speak to about things that have been kept buried or secret for long periods. In this process there can be a release of painful emotions as a kind of by-product of being free to speak about difficult experiences.

What the reflective process tends to do, however, is separate us from a direct relationship to what we are feeling. We may touch in to our feelings and then rapidly move away into conceptual reflection because it is more comfortable. We can then remain in the realm of our conceptual mind rather than staying in immediate relationship to our feelings. This may seem like a good thing if we actually want to be away from our feelings; however, I know from my therapeutic work as well as my own experience that continual conceptual reflection, analyzing feelings, does not necessarily resolve them, because the roots go very deep.

In the therapy setting, this has been very noticeable in the way clients respond to their emotional life. It is also easy for a therapist to perpetuate this separating from feelings by the tendency to become too interested in talking about the story of feelings. Feelings can then be kept at an apparently safe distance for both the therapist and the client. While talking about our problems in therapy does have its benefits as a means of expressing what is going on and gaining clarity and understanding, we should also recognize its limitations. Unfortunately, it does not always change deep-rooted emotional wounding. To do so we need to be in actual relationship to its feeling; we need a quality of presence.

As a working psychotherapist, I have found that the move to remaining present in relation to feeling has been extremely important when working with clients going through deep distress. Unfortunately, not everyone is ready or able to stay with feelings, and many would rather talk about them from a somewhat disconnected place. The problem is that it is then possible to go on and on about how we are feeling and yet not truly feel the feelings and consequently never really change anything. Being willing to stay in relationship to feelings, however, means a shift of attention from reflecting upon them to simply being present with them.

Within the therapeutic setting, psychotherapists have become increasingly aware of this problem and so learn during their training to help people to stay with their feelings, to experience them directly and fully so that they can release and change. This does not, as some might fear, lead to becoming stuck in feelings that are very uncomfortable; learning to be with them enables them to move on. Witnessing and being present with feelings having an awareness that is free of conceptual thinking takes courage and needs to be learned. This is where some of the understanding gained from Buddhist meditation can be extremely helpful. What has become apparent over the past twenty years or so is that a way of awareness developed in meditation is increasingly being brought into the therapeutic context. The particular examples of this more-contemplative style are found in the more-body-centered psychotherapies as well as in what is called Focusing and mindfulness-based therapy.

The shift from reflection to presence takes us through a number of stages. With each stage we come more intimately into relationship with our felt experience such that it can be transformed more and more fully. One of the central ingredients in this process is a greater emphasis on our relationship to the body. From a psychological perspective, the deeper relationship to the nature of our feeling and emotional life cannot be separated from the body, as they are intimately connected. The implication of this in terms of the shift from reflection to presence is that as we move toward presence, the body is clearly the basic ground of our experience.

Drawing on both his Buddhist and his psychotherapeutic background, John Welwood has made some important clarifications on this deepening process, which I have depicted in figure 4 on page 67.[2] We can see in this map that at the starting point we have little capacity for reflecting objectively upon our experience but that once this reflection begins, we have an in-creased ability to know ourselves. It is the gradual movement from a conceptual reflection toward the threshold of present awareness that is so often used in therapy. Here we can use the Focusing approach, which places awareness in direct relation-ship to felt experiences and then uses our capacity to name or find an image for these feelings to open up their meaning and understanding. When focusing we do not analyze and reflect upon our feelings, we simply allow a word, phrase, or image to come, and then we return to relationship with the feelings themselves. This process itself can be very liberating in its ef-fect upon the nature of feelings. They are naturally allowed to be what they are without our trying to make them into some kind of story. When left in this way, they start to evolve and move on. The focusing process enables a very subtle dialogue with felt experience.

As we go deeper and move across the threshold into the territory of presence, we begin to witness our felt experi-ences with less and less conceptual chatter about them. This journey will require a more meditative style that enables us to quieten the thinking mind and settle in the body with its feeling life. Mindfulness is a key factor in this process as we become more and more able to witness what is arising with-out becoming identified with it and getting pulled by it or lost in it. Mindfulness from a Tibetan point of view is simply the capacity to hold our mind upon an object of awareness. In Tibetan the word *trenba,* or mindfulness, actually means "to remember." Mindfulness, then, is the capacity to hold the mind on an object and maintain that awareness. This capac-ity is paired with another important ability, alertness, where we recognize that we have wandered off. As we meditate with our awareness increasingly held on our feeling life, when we drift off into some thought process, alertness recognizes this fact and mindfulness brings us back.

The great advantage of mindfulness as it is beginning to be used in the therapeutic setting is that it can help people to see, for the first time, their emotional states in a clearer, witnessed way. Rather than drowning in painful emotions like despair and depression, they are able to witness them and allow them to move through. This is rather like lifting our head up out of the water so we can breathe again. It allows our sense of self to be separate from the strength of feeling without splitting off from it or pushing it away. Witnessing emotions and feelings frees us to be our normal self again, not taken over, which is especially important with painful feelings of depression or despair or grief. It can also help us listen to our feelings and discern what we need and what is beneficial in our emotional life so that we can be more congruent in how we respond to the world. The capacity to witness this process will also enable us to see when we are caught in projected illusions. The world will begin to come back into focus again, and we will see through some of our deluded views. We can begin to see that perhaps things are not so bad, we are not so hopeless, people are not so unpleasant—not because they have changed but because we have stopped projecting.

Mindfulness, however, can have two dimensions to it, one that is very focused on something specific and one that is more spacious and open. As we allow our awareness to become more spacious, we settle increasingly into the mind's natural clarity and presence. It is at this point that presence begins to have

its significance as a way of being with feelings and emotions
with bare awareness. Within the Tibetan tradition, the practice that is intended to enable this quality of bare awareness is
known as Mahamudra. In that approach to meditation on the
nature of the mind itself—or perhaps one could say, the natural state of awareness—bare awareness becomes increasingly
refined as well as spacious and open. Eventually we become
able simply to rest in the mind's natural clarity and spaciousness free of conceptual disturbance.

While at first the presence of bare awareness has a subtle
witness that can act as a focus of attention within the larger
field of awareness, gradually this witness will fade until we are
left with a state of nondual awareness or nondual presence.
Within this sphere of awareness, feelings may arise and pass,
images may come and go, and thoughts may float through, but
they are not discriminated as things in their own right. They do
not disturb the natural clarity of awareness. Eventually they are
seen as simply movements of the mind's clarity and luminosity.

With the practice of Mahamudra we become able to allow
our emotional processes to come and go as they will, without
our being so caught up in their charge and the need to create
form around them. While the reflective process is associated
with naming our experiences and giving them form, the Mahamudra approach is a kind of unnaming that releases them from
the movement into form. This absence of a formation tension
leaves the energy of the emotion to emerge, transform, and
return to the clarity from which it came—like the clouds that
emerge from the blue sky, which have no home and which return to the sky whence they came.[3] Emotions become liberated
in their own nature of emptiness and clarity.

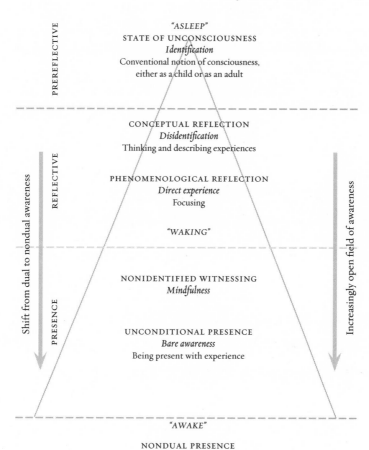

FIG. 4. *Map of the evolution of consciousness, based on John Welwood,* Toward a Psychology of Awakening *(Boston: Shambhala Publications, 2002).*

The gradual shift from the process of reflection to that of presence requires much time and practice. It is also easier to do if we have some experience of meditation. While some aspects of the shift to presence through practices such as Focusing can be done in relation to another person in one-to-one therapy, the deeper levels of presence are primarily accessed within the domain of meditation. It is nevertheless the deeper level that can have a profoundly liberating effect on the entire process of our emotional life. Once this quality of present awareness begins to be cultivated, it is one of the most important discoveries in our relationship to our emotional life.

8

learning to be
with feelings

WHEN I WAS YOUNGER AND was experiencing painful and often strong feelings and emotions, my tendency to be caught in my head would not shift my emotional
state. I would think about my feelings and become caught up
in a great amount of angst about them but could not often resolve them. When I had strong feelings or emotions, I would
often find myself overwhelmed by them, and no amount of
trying to think differently about them helped. What I needed
was a way of meditation that would enable me to be in relationship to my feeling life with a greater capacity to witness what
was arising rather than be overwhelmed by it. Greater orientation toward feeling as a dominant aspect of life should not
be seen as wrong or antithetical to Buddhist understanding.

It can mean that those who are involved in Buddhist practice may need to orient their approach in a subtly different way. What I recognized was that the Tibetan tradition in which I grew up did not particularly emphasize the style of meditation I needed. There was more emphasis on a conceptual process than on meditation. It was my discovery of the practice of Mahamudra, however, that eventually began to make a difference. While this is the meditation found within the Tibetan tradition, it has much in common with meditations found in other traditions of Buddhism, such as the Theravada practice of Vipassana.

I was first guided into the practice of Mahamudra by Lama Thubten Yeshe, who had a background that combined the Buddhist philosophy on emptiness with the teachings on the nature of mind more commonly found within Nyingma *dzogchen* and Kagyu Mahamudra.[1] I found that it was this approach to the nature of mind in meditation that enabled a way of being with my emotions and feelings that was practical and immediate. Furthermore, it got me out of my head and back into my body and feelings in a healthier way. What I found especially important was learning to allow feelings to be as they are without trying to do something to them. I began to discover that when I have the capacity to remain with an open and spacious awareness, emotions and feelings can arise and simply move through as a flow of energy, going where it needs to go. This requires a kind of "nonstick" awareness that doesn't react to a feeling by contracting into it or pushing it away. It is also a quality of mind that does not go into the torrent of thoughts that are often stirred by strong feelings, where one often judges them in some way or gets caught in their story.

Having described in general terms in the previous chapter the shift from a reflective mind to one that is just quietly present, I would now like to describe some of the aspects of this process within the practice of Mahamudra meditation.

Mahamudra is a style of meditation that cultivates the capacity to rest in the natural clarity of awareness, the nature of the mind. It is often considered to be one of the most advanced practices in the tantric tradition, but there is also great value in aspects of this practice that can be developed without engaging in tantric practice. Mahamudra can be extremely beneficial for those who are relative beginners of meditation practice as well as for more-advanced practitioners. In essence, with Mahamudra we cultivate a quality of clear, present, spacious awareness, but that is not easy to do at first because the mind is such a subtle, illusive object, and the normal discursive chatter and business of the ordinary mind are so strong and difficult to pacify. Consequently, we need to move toward this experience in gradual stages.

To be able to rest eventually in the natural clarity of the mind, we must first of all begin to settle our awareness. The most beneficial way to do this is by developing the quality of mindfulness by resting on the natural arising and passing of the breath. Breath awareness was one of the most basic and profound practices taught by the Buddha in the sutra known as Anapanasati, and it is the foundation for the practice of mindfulness.[2] The cultivation of awareness upon the breath can be done in a variety of ways, but what I would suggest here is to bring attention to the sensations of the breath as felt in the rising of the in-breath and the settling, descending of the out-breath. It is really helpful to keep an awareness of the subtle sensations of the breath, noticing their varying qualities of strength and smoothness.

In the practice of Mahamudra, it is helpful to give attention to the quality of the out-breath as a natural relaxing and settling down of the body. This brings the center of gravity of awareness out of the head and down toward the lower part of the body. We should retain this process of breath awareness as long as is needed to deepen and relax the mind into a quietened state. To accomplish this, we need to continually bring attention back to the sensation of breathing whenever it is drawn away by thoughts.

Once our mind settles on the sensations of the breath in this way, we can gradually open awareness into the sensations and feelings throughout the body. This can begin with the trunk of the body and then progress out into the limbs. This is where we begin to let the mind settle in sensation and feelings with bare awareness, an awareness that is free of the conceptual habit of reflecting upon the content of our awareness. While doing this, it is helpful to retain an awareness of the breath, breathing in with an awareness of feeling and sensation and breathing out with an awareness of feeling and sensation. It is as though the feelings and sensations in the entire body were breathing.

To become aware of the sensations and feelings in the body, it can be helpful to start with what is often called a body-sweep meditation. This involves gradually sweeping awareness from the crown down through the body, part by part, so that eventually we wake up an awareness of the entire body. It is very helpful to do this process carefully and slowly so that we really do wake up awareness in parts of the body that may feel asleep. Once we have swept awareness down through the body, we can expand attention to the entire body and then remain with this awareness for as long as possible. This practice takes time to cultivate if it is unfamiliar, in which case it is worth repeating the meditation many times. Once familiar this body sweep can be done relatively briefly.

Resting in body sensation with bare awareness free of discursive mental conceptions enables us to stop interfering mentally with our experience: giving things labels and in some subtle way evaluating our feelings. We gradually develop the facility to witness the arising and passing of feelings and emotions without contracting into them or pushing them away. Gaining this equanimity in relation to the arising of feelings means we do not get sticky around them and can let them unravel in the space of awareness, accepting whatever feelings arise.

With the practice of Mahamudra we gradually develop the capacity to remain with a spacious presence within feelings and emotions. Some approaches to this kind of practice can be extremely focused, giving attention to particular feelings and watching how they unfold and what kind of intentions arise from them. It is not this way with Mahamudra, at least not at first. We are sitting with more spaciousness around feelings, letting them unfold without getting too intensely concentrated upon them. We are learning to hold awareness in a lighter, more-relaxed way, and this spaciousness allows feelings room to open out and be released.

This capacity to remain present and aware of feelings and emotions is not yet the eventual practice of Mahamudra, but it is movement in that direction. If we do not first have this capacity to be with feeling and sensation, it is highly possible for meditators who come to rest immediately in the nature of mind to bypass their emotional life in an unhealthy way. This does not enable us either to be with or to transform our emotions. Instead it perpetuates the tendency to dissociate from them. Something that has often concerned me in the process of mentoring is encountering people who have been guided to experience the mind's clarity in a very disconnected way, out of relationship to both feelings and the body. This somewhat spaced-out tendency needs to be countered if real transformation of our feeling reality is to arise.

If we return to the map of feelings in chapter 3, we can see how the deepening experience of present awareness will help us relate to the spectrum of feelings. With this awareness we can for the first time potentially disidentify from the strength of emotions as they arise. This means we are able to witness stronger emotions and retain a clear sense of self rather than becoming submerged in the emotion. This is the basis of mindfulness, a practice now being used within the therapeutic world that is increasingly valuable in helping people to gain this witnessing of emotions rather than being lost in them. This has become especially valuable for people suffering painful feelings of despair and depression.

Present awareness particularly comes into its own when we move into the subtler domain of our feeling life. This can be the best way to listen to our feelings without actually having to do something with them. We learn simply to remain present with the ebb and flow of feeling tones, giving space for them to go where they naturally go. What this increased awareness enables is a capacity not to become caught in feelings that would otherwise become stronger emotions. We catch them before they turn into storm clouds. This also means that we are able to recognize the pleasant, unpleasant, and neutral feelings with a greater capacity of disidentification and objectivity. Witnessing their arising and passing stops us from reacting in relation to them; it also gives us a level of insight into our experiences. Particularly, we see the impermanent, ephemeral, moment-to-moment arising of our experiences.

Becoming more settled and spacious in our awareness, we can gradually rest in the territory of what we can call a felt sense. This more-diffuse feeling tone is the ground from which our more-distinct feelings emerge. This increasing capacity to rest in and listen to our feeling life also facilitates a process of focusing now used frequently in the therapy world. There are many books written about this subject, so I will not go into great detail here. Briefly, however, when focusing, once we are able to rest in the more-diffuse felt sense of the body, we begin to pay attention to a particular subtle quality of feeling and allow it to convey some sense of meaning or information to us. If, for example, I become aware of a particular feeling in one area of the body, I may settle into it and then allow an image or phrase to come that conveys a sense of its quality. We do not need to analyze the feeling and go into a reflective process, which takes us further away from the feeling. Rather, we notice what arises around it and then return to the awareness of the feeling itself. This may then begin to change and bring out some other level of feeling. Repeating this process enables us to truly listen to the emergence of our felt response to our life. It becomes a source of great insight and understanding of how we are in the world.

Resting in our felt sense, we begin to lose some of the disposition to contract into the stronger feelings and instead remain open and spacious. It is on this level of awareness that we
may also become aware of subtle aspects of the environment
in which we move. This may be in a group of people, but it
could equally be in the natural world. The experience of our
felt sense can open us to the experience of others' feelings in a
way that can be both beneficial and sometimes disturbing. The
greater sensitivity that comes with this kind of awareness is a
mixed blessing. Those who have this capacity will often need
to differentiate what is coming from the environment and the
people they associate with from what is actually their own. It is
often at this level that those who have in some way been abused
or whose boundaries have been emotionally violated will have
huge sensitivity. This sensitivity was always there underneath
but often in a way that was debilitating, frightening, and confusing. When I consider some of the people I have worked
with in therapy, I realize that this disposition to be extremely
sensitive to the environment has often led to a kind of hyper-
vigilance. It can easily lead to feeling very unsafe much of the
time, and any subtle and unconscious aggression in people they
encounter can be extremely disturbing. It can also lead to being confused as to whose "stuff" they are feeling. This can be
doubly difficult because the people they sense are often not
aware of what they are doing, so the experience cannot easily
be verified. With meditation and skill, it becomes possible to
make this differentiation clearer and be able to separate out
self from other.

There are other examples of this sensitivity that make the
relationship to the natural world very alive and interesting.

One person I have worked with for many years has found this of great importance. Working particularly in the natural environment has enabled a sensitivity to the land and the presence of elemental energies there to deepen, bringing a rich and healing experience. Working in this way enables another person I have supervised to take people through some important processes of transformation within the natural world.

If we allow ourselves to go deeper and open still further, we begin to feel into the underlying vitality and energy of the ground of our feeling life. As we move into this territory, we are less bound up by the turmoil of emotions and feelings and instead touch the subtle energetic nature of the mind as a felt tone. This deepened sensitivity moves us into a field of experience where inner and outer distinctions become less clear. Our own vitality and subtle energy and that of the natural environment cannot really be separated once we rest in this level of experience.

Returning to the process of the actual practice of Mahamudra: once we become increasingly settled in subtle levels of feelings or the felt sense, there is a small shift of attention we can begin to make. This shift begins to happen naturally but can also be helped more consciously. Up to this point we are still aware of feeling as the object of our attention. There is a subtle subject-object splitting going on. At any point in this process, we can gently relax and open our awareness out a little and rest back in the quality of present awareness itself. This is not to separate our awareness from feeling but to become aware of the spacious sense of presence within which it arises. We will see that feeling is not other than the nature of awareness, and awareness is not other than the nature of feeling. We recognize that awareness, or the nature of mind, and this subtle level of feeling are what might be described as coemergent. They cannot really be differentiated as subject and object anymore. The mind's natural clarity and brightness are pervaded by the felt experience of something deeply pleasant and potentially blissful, although it may not be fully experienced in this way at this point.

We are now beginning to rest in the nature of mind that is the aim of Mahamudra practice. This practice can be developed still further as our capacity to rest in clear awareness becomes more stable and free of the obstructions of agitation and dullness. This is the cultivation of what is called in Sanskrit *shamatha* (Tib., *shinay*), or tranquil abiding.

In Mahamudra this deepening ability to settle in quiet awareness then leads to a further capacity to explore the nature of what arises within awareness. This is the development of what is called vipassana, or insight. It is within the process of vipassana that we examine specifically the nature of our experiences. We may begin by exploring the nature of feelings and sensations, seeing their fleeting, impermanent, and empty nature. We may watch the arising of thoughts and images and recognize that they are also fleeting and in nature appearances of the mind, in the same way that clouds emerge from the sky. We can then turn to the mind itself, recognizing it to be empty of inherent and enduring substantiality. This exploration is not done through conceptual analysis, as it is in some Tibetan traditions,[3] but, rather, through a more direct investigation similar to shining a flashlight into a room with a particular intention. In the Mahamudra commentary by the Dalai Lama, it is described as being like a fish that explores the water without disturbing its clarity.⁴ The mind is then seen to have no enduring or substantial characteristics; it has no form or color. It is just awareness empty of inherent nature. Again, once this experience of the empty nature of mind is stabilized, the meditator looks more directly into the way in which other appearances exist. Within Mahamudra a particular awareness dawns, that all of these appearances are seen to arise from the natural clarity of the mind itself, or the clear-light mind, and this clear-light mind is by nature empty.

As we see, the practice of Mahamudra meditation can take us deeper and deeper into our experience. What I found so important about the early stages of Mahamudra is that they were the answer to the struggle I was consistently caught in when I was younger. I could not be with my feeling and emotional life. It consistently took me over, and I found myself lost within it, and the pain and confusion that it would bring were hard to cope with. These initial experiences of the Mahamudra practice are extremely valuable in that it they give us one of the most potent tools for being with our feeling life: a basic quality of awareness. If we become particularly adept in this way, our practice will go deeper and deeper, with far-reaching benefits. It will also enable us to see the nature of our sense of self in a very different way.

creating
inner space

ONCE WE DEEPEN OUR capacity to meditate within the territory of sensations and feelings, together with their underlying energy/vitality, we begin to see some important aspects of our sense of self, which has two dimensions. One is a natural capacity to hold a relatively stable sense of self-identity in our relationship to the experiences of our inner and outer life. This self acts as a filter and focus for what we are going through from moment to moment, and without it we would find it extremely difficult to focus our subjective life. We would be disintegrated and scattered in relation to the events of our life. Effectively, without a sense of self, we would become extremely disoriented and psychologically unstable, potentially leading to psychosis.

Alongside—or perhaps one could say within—the emergence of this healthy sense of self as we grow up, there also grows another tendency. This is a gradual solidification of self into something that feels very real, solid, and central to who we are. I say "feels" because this is not an intellectual or philosophical notion of a self, a me, or an I; it is a felt "me." Modern psychology has become increasingly clear that this process of constellating a sense of self begins very early on, even, some would say, within the womb. It is the influences of the environment as they impact the fetus and then the infant after birth that gradually mold a sense of me that seems solid and real. This, of course, is not described within Buddhist philosophy in any depth because Buddhism does not propose a developmental model.

In Buddhist philosophy a great deal of time may be spent analyzing the nature of the I, but that does not alter the fact that as we experience it, it is felt. It will, of course, have a mental component that holds on to a conception of me that has certain beliefs about itself. I recall going through hours of self-reflective introspection as an adolescent, trying to decide who or what I was, but this was not very helpful. What was happening organically, in spite of me, was the gradual establishment of my "identity project" with these two dimensions of the self, one the natural relative self and the other the more emotional solid self, growing in parallel.[1] From a Buddhist point of view, these two dimensions form our self-identity or self-image, our sense of me.

What we recognize in our exploration of this phenomenon from a psychological perspective is that the felt experience of me becomes focused around a number of things. One is the sense of our body and how we feel about ourselves as body. Another is the more superficial view we have of ourselves as our self-image and self-identity grow. There is also a deeper sense of whether we feel okay about ourselves or not that grows from a very early period of development and profoundly colors our sense of self. This is the sense of me that comes up when we are hurt or upset. It is this emotionally charged sense of me that can become clearer when we sit in meditation and feel into it.

Furthermore, the beliefs we hold around our sense of self become very solid, as though they were "true." This means that feeling "I am not good enough" or "I am not lovable" or "I am ugly" and so on all become concrete identifications that we hold as true and solidly existent. Essentially, they can feel very substantial and real. When someone does something to aggravate us or we are confronted with certain difficult circumstances, a vivid sense of me arises that feels completely real and solid. The particular beliefs we then have about ourself will also be extremely painful to feel. Feeling one is not good enough, for example, can bring with it an appalling sense of despair or self-hatred.

A woman I have seen as a client described how she was asked to give a talk at a conference. Although she was extremely accomplished in the topic she was asked to speak on, what came up for her was an intense fear and feeling of inadequacy. She did give the talk, and it was very successful, but then afterward she was full of self-recrimination, partly because she was unable to let in the positive response from the audience. She described the intense sense of contraction into a vivid feeling of "me" and the painful feelings of self-loathing.

What seemed so hard for her was that she had such an intense feeling that this negative sense of self was true, unchanging, and solid. She had spent many years doing work on herself, but this ego-contracted, painful self-belief seemed to be so solid and enduring.

This solidification of a sense of me is, from a Buddhist point of view, the essential ingredient of ignorance. This is the ignorance that grasps at the self as truly existent and colors all the emotional reactions that then emerge. Basically all of our suffering arises from grasping at the self as though it were real, solid, and enduring. This contraction into a sense of me as real is called in Tibetan *dagtsin,* or ego grasping, and is considered to be the primary factor that is at the root of all the suffering we experience in our life. In this respect, it is not having a sense of self that is the problem; it is ego grasping, the contracted sense of self. This is an important distinction that even some Buddhists fail to grasp. When the phrase *no self* or *emptiness of self* is expressed, it is to say that there is no substantial, enduring self, not that there is no relative self. As I said earlier, we need a robust and stable sense of relative self.

To overcome this disposition of ego grasping, we need to look very closely at the habit. If and when we recognize the tendency and see clearly the sense of me that is vividly appearing and held as solid, then we can begin to change the habit of contraction and grasping. This is where meditation is very helpful.

In the Tibetan tradition, there are two distinct methods for looking at this ego-grasping experience. One is a more intellectual analysis and the other is based on direct experience. The intellectual form relies on an analysis of whether we can find an I or a me anywhere in the body or mind by dissecting every aspect of who we are. One would continue to reflect upon whether the various components of the body—for example, legs, arms, skin, or muscles—can be an I until one realizes intellectually that there is no place for an I to dwell. This intellectual recognition would then be meditated upon for as long as possible in the hope that meditation would translate an intellectual idea into an experience.

Having spent many of my early years as a Tibetan Buddhist with this approach, I can appreciate the intellectual rigor and effectiveness of analysis. What I have never found is that it easily translates into a direct experience that cuts through the felt sense of me. I always valued the intellectual understanding this analysis gave, but I needed to approach it from a different direction.

It is in the practice of meditation that this different direction can be found. If we return to the kind of Mahamudra meditation I referred to in the previous chapter, we find that what it is initially oriented toward is resting with a quiet present awareness within the experience of feeling and sensations within the body. Of course, our experience of me is predominantly felt within the body, although if we are, for example, worrying about something, then the felt sense of me is likely to be in the head.

This meditation upon the feelings and sensations in the body brings us to see that our experience of life within the body and feelings is in constant flux. The very changing, fluid nature of feelings and sensations and the energy within them become more and more apparent as we sit quietly and witness them. We can become aware on a very subtle level of the

arising and passing of feelings. We can equally feel the movement of the energy around the body, and the more we settle,
the more we will feel the quality of the organs and the fluids
that move through them as less and less solid.

Sitting in meditation with a mind that is not caught in
discursive chatter enables a clearer sense of the process that
makes up who we are. We start to see with bare awareness
that we are actually just a process unfolding. This process is
the basis of the sense of me. Upon this process we put the
label that is our name. I am just a process with the label Rob
on it. The point of this is that as we sit quietly and directly
experience the fluidity of our inner life, we can use a very
subtle and unintrusive investigation simply to look and see if
there is anything that is the basis of an enduring, solid sense
of me. This investigation is like shining a flashlight around in
a cave to see if there is anything living there.

The beauty of this approach is that we are already in a
deep and steady state of meditation before we investigate.
Indeed, it is not really possible to do this investigation unless we already have a steady meditation state largely free of
discursive thoughts. It also means that we do not need to
move into the intellectual, conceptual mind to analyze our
experience.

Once we have gone through this process, we can do the
same, if we wish, with any experience other than looking for
"me" that arises in the mind, such as images and thoughts,
to see if there is a me there that is abiding and solid. Finally,
we can look at the mind itself to see if there is any enduring
quality. What we will recognize is that although there is defi-
nitely a quality of awareness, we cannot find it in the past, the

present, or the future. It has no shape, color, or location. It is therefore no basis on which an enduring solid me can exist.

Meditation in this way leads to a more spacious sense of present awareness, once we begin to rest and open our awareness around the experience of "no me." If we can relax our mind in that state, it will enable us to let go of the disposition to contract and tighten into a sense of me when it arises. This doesn't mean the sense of me will not arise, but it does mean that as it arises, we simply allow it to be a transitory part of the process that is moving through. When something stimulates a sense of me and the inclination grows to contract into it and solidify our sense of self, instead we can remain more spacious and open. As we do this, we will slowly free ourselves of many of the narrow, emotionally charged patterns that are so bound up in the wounded sense of me.

In the Tibetan meditation practice called *chöd,* a meditator goes into a scary place to invoke a vivid sense of me based on fear. Traditionally this would have included places such as charnel grounds where it was believed that there were a lot of spirits present. I once visited such a wild place in India and had no doubt that it would have been very challenging to stay there alone. It certainly provoked a strong reaction in me that brought up that vivid sense of "me." When this sense of I is clearly identified, the mind cuts through the root of ego grasping; hence the term *chöd:* literally, "to cut." In principle we do not need to go to special places to give rise to the vivid sense of I, because it arises frequently in our daily life. It arises when we are driving and someone annoys us. It arises when we are eagerly anticipating getting something in a shop, only to find the item has sold out. It arises when we drive through speed

cameras or receive a parking ticket. There are so many circumstances in our day that can potentially bring up the strong
sense of me, especially when we feel anger or irritation.

When we have a clear sense of this me to be negated, we
are in a good position to use the meditation I have described
very easily. Without first identifying this solid, vivid me or I,
we may end up negating the normal functional me that is a
necessary part of our identity. As we differentiate the two and
lessen the contraction into the me that does not actually exist,
we will begin to feel a greater sense of inner space as we are
freed from some of the emotional reactions that can dominate
our life.

Once we are able to rest in the clarity of present awareness with the spaciousness that comes from seeing clearly the
absence of a solid me, our experience of feelings changes. We
could say that there is no longer an experiencer, a feeler, and
yet there can be a subtle witness of simply the arising and
passing of feeling, sensation, and, indeed, emotions within
the space of awareness. In time even the duality of the witness
drops away and we are left with the clear spacious sense of
nonduality within which whatever arises returns to its natural state of emptiness. There is just the flux of feeling and
sensation as they arise and pass within the space of clarity and
emptiness. What this leads us to is the recognition that we are
just a process with a label ME upon it. We will see that there
are feelings without a solid, permanent feeler.

Part Two

emotional
integrity

10

transforming
the emotions

As we begin to explore ways in which we might transform our emotional life, we will discover many different approaches, both in the world of Western psychology and in Buddhism. From my own exploration, I have seen that there are some interesting similarities between the two, and there can also appear to be some apparent contradictions that are not easily resolved. To reiterate something I suggested earlier: in my initial relationship to the Tibetan tradition of Buddhism, I frequently encountered the view that seemed to designate all emotions as "emotional afflictions" that are essentially a problem to be overcome. As delusions, they are an aspect of the mind that gives rise to karma and therefore are the basis of suffering. In this view, great emphasis is placed, as Shantideva saw it, upon never bowing down to "disturbing conceptions" because they are the demons that lead us to the lower realms. From this point of view it would seem that all emotional afflictions need to be pacified; then one will be free to experience inner peace. The primary means of pacification is the application of opposing antidotes that neutralize the negative mind by introducing positive states.

With this view it is easy to consider that all emotions are afflictions and therefore destructive and to be overcome. There is no differentiation of appropriate emotion or any innate value in emotion. As I indicated earlier, one of the reasons this confusion can arise is that there is no equivalent term in Tibetan for what we refer to as emotion. The translation of the Tibetan term *nyonmong* as "delusion" or "emotional affliction" does not help in this process. This more-traditional view of emotions, however, is becoming somewhat modified and developed by those who, in bringing together Buddhist and Western psychology, see that this is perhaps too simplistic. Our emotional life is a little more complex than the view of emotions as just destructive delusions would imply.

It is in association with the Western psychotherapeutic and healing world that we find a view that seemingly contradicts the traditional Buddhist view. Here it is generally considered that emotions and feelings, in all of their diversity, are a natural expression of our relationship to life and that healthy or appropriate emotion is a desirable condition. This is not to say that all emotions are beneficial but that they are often a natural response to aspects of our life. In this respect, if I did not experience fear when in danger or grief at a time of loss or anger if I am being abused, this would probably be unhealthy. Many emotions are part of a natural play of our experience that are a necessary presence for health. With this view we might consider that unless we genuinely embrace our emotions fully, we cannot experience the richness and happiness life can bring. Equally, if we are unable to relate to the nuances of our feeling and emotional life, life will become arid and without real engagement and meaning. Our relationships will become mechanical and uncaring. What makes the emotions problematic is the excessive or overwhelming and unconscious dominance of emotions such as anger, aggression, jealousy, pride, desire, fear, and so on that then become potentially destructive and need to be brought into balance.

Within both the world of therapy and healing and Buddhist thinking, therefore, it could be said that it is not the emotions per se that are unhealthy but the way we respond or relate to them. When we do not relate to them openly and allow them to be as they are to move through us, we become bound up with them in an unhealthy way, and they become what we might call an affliction. When we go unconscious, become overwhelmed, or block and suppress an emotion, it becomes unhealthy. It can then dominate us and become destructive to both us and others. This means that we can begin to distinguish between emotion itself as a natural expression of our feeling life and the secondary contraction into an unhealthy relationship we may have with our emotions.

It is therefore not necessarily the presence of an emotion that is the problem but how we respond to it. Fear, anger, sadness, grief, desire, disappointment, and the like can all be natural expressions of our everyday experience of relating to the world; the question will be how we respond to these feelings.

If we hold the view that such feelings are always wrong and should be overcome, then the danger with "overcoming" is that it will often mean repression. This could imply that someone who has this view within his or her spiritual practice could end up in a straitjacket on the surface but with a great deal of suppressed emotion beneath. Is this what is intended in Buddhist life? Is our emotional life to be abandoned or integrated healthily?

This question is important when we begin to consider the idea of transforming the emotions. Of course, a lot of our emotional life is uncomfortable, distressing, and painful, and we want it to be different. We may wish to be rid of it; we may fear it, judge it, and find it unacceptable. The idea of transformation does not imply that emotions are going to be gotten rid of but that through a different relationship to them, something does begin to change. The danger with the idea of transformation could be the attitude that rejects emotions and tries to turn them into something else that is acceptable. There is a paradox in this process. Aversion to emotions does not transform them. Often what needs to be transformed is not the emotions themselves but our way of being with them.

Transformation means first of all recognizing that emotions are as they are, a natural process of our felt relationship to life situations. If we can then begin to open to them fully, without fear, resistance, or aversion, we can stay in relationship to them. If we can then gradually counter the disposition to contract and grasp at them or box them up and push them away, they will have a way of unfolding naturally. To do this we will need to have the kind of witness awareness that I spoke of previously. It helps to have the clarity that does not

Contraction is self contraction

become caught in the conceptual, mental confusion that tends to be generated around our emotions. We can then remain open to the nature of the emotional process and allow it to pass through us in a more embodied way.

In transforming our emotions, we also need to remember that at the heart of our emotional life is the tendency to contract into a tight and solid feeling of me. Indeed, our emotions contribute hugely to the flavor of our wounded ego grasping. From a Buddhist point of view, ego grasping is central to the manifestation of and our response to our emotional life. If we have a strong disposition to contract into a very solid sense of me, then the way we experience emotions will become equally intense. What turns an emotional process into something that takes us over is the degree to which we contract into the sense of me. We can then get caught in an intense feeling of me within the emotion. When we are able to loosen and soften that solidity of ego contraction we will not become so caught in the power of the emotions. With a more spacious and permeable sense of self, the impact of emotions is not so strong, and they can flow through us more fluidly.

In Buddhist philosophy it is considered that if we cut through this habit of ego contraction, the delusions that are the secondary process will begin to fall away. Does this mean that we suddenly have no emotional or feeling response to life situations? Or does it mean that the emotional experiences we have will be less intense because the contracted root of suffering is not present? If someone has experienced emptiness of self and has little or no contraction of self-grasping, does the person still experience emotions of sadness, grief, anger—or equally, joy, elation, love, care, and compassion? My sense of this is, Why not? There is still a conventional self that relates to experiences and feels some of them as painful and others as meaningful or beautiful. The difference is that the contraction into the painful state of affliction of feeling and emotion is not happening. It is still possible to be assertive and state one's boundaries without the contracted ego grasping. It is still possible to experience the sadness and distress of seeing someone in great pain and suffering. It is still possible to feel deeply the sense of awe and beauty of a mountain landscape. As the psychotherapist and Buddhist practitioner Mark Epstein indicates, it is also still possible to experience desire, because it is not the desire that is the problem; desire simply moves us toward an intention.[1] It is the contraction into ego grasping that turns these feelings into attachment and suffering.

When we take the ego contraction out of our experience, our emotional life can still remain alive and rich but without the tight, stuck, obsessive sense of me that ego grasping brings. Things flow through more freely and with less obstruction and judgment, perhaps also with less drama and intensity. They are as they are, they arise and pass through, and we are left enriched, whether they are painful or pleasant. Our emotions are part of our capacity to embrace our life fully, with a sense of its value and meaning, and not run away from it or avoid it. When we embrace life in this way, we will experience the pain of certain situations and the joy and beauty of others. This will become a basis of suffering only when we become fixed and obsessive and contract, cling, and grasp at our experiences and feelings. If we can remain open and spacious, emotions can begin to be liberated, because like everything else, they are empty of any solid, enduring nature.

In the *dzogchen* tradition, the emotions are allowed to be as they are, and when experienced in the awareness of nonduality, they become self-liberated. In Mahamudra the emotions are the play of the mind's intrinsic vitality and luminosity when they are seen in their true nature as empty of any solid self-existence. In this way the emotions are the very basis of our wisdom when we see their innate nature directly.

What we may begin to see as we become more comfortable with this emotional unfolding is that within the energy of the emotions is a natural wisdom that is innate to our nature. When I consider emotions such as fear, I can see that on one hand I could tighten into a sense of self that is to my detriment. I can become taken over by the fear, and it then becomes a kind of affliction. I could, alternatively, stay open to the fear and let its energy move through me. Then it brings a sense of vivid alertness that is extremely important in life.

When I lived in retreat high above McLeod Ganj in the northern India Himalayas, I was very aware of bears in my environment. They had occasionally killed cattle on the mountainside around my retreat hut at night and sadly on one occasion they had killed a small boy who was the son of a shepherd. Each night I would need to walk out of my safe retreat courtyard to go and take a pee. The nights were very dark in the mountains, and every evening I would have a strong rush of fear as I walked to my peeing spot. I knew that bears were very quick, and my fantasy was that they would attack from behind.

There were occasions when I could feel the buzz of adrenaline turn into a powerful fear and flight reaction that would compel me to rush back to the safety of my hut. On other occasions, if I stayed really open and relaxed and felt the energy of the fear arise and move through me, the quality of sharp alertness was acute. My senses were very alive, and I was instantly alert to the slightest sound. It was an extraordinarily alive state of clarity and vividness that would clearly be of immense natural value if I were an animal in the wild with predators around.

Within our emotion is a natural wisdom that can be discovered only when we are really open, with clarity and awareness, to the core of the felt experience. Anger is another example where, if I can stay with the feeling when it arises and not become caught in the contracted state of affliction, it moves right through me. Then I discover the natural quality of intention and wisdom that lies within it. In my own life I notice that when anger arises, if I can truly be open to its presence, I see deep within it a sense of powerlessness and vulnerability that often accompanies certain situations. When I can come into relationship with the intensity of the anger in its essential nature, I see my need to assert something, perhaps a boundary, or to affect something and make it unfold. Possibly the single most-noticeable cause that gives rise to anger in my own life is my experience of chaos. When I look deeply into this feeling, I recognize again my sense of powerlessness. If I can be fully open to the feelings this brings, then I have a choice. I can either begin to do something to clear the chaos, or I can choose to let go and live with it. Within this entire process I learn the wisdom innate within the dynamic of anger.

All of us will discover what it is we learn as we open more fully to the emotions we have. If we remain on the surface of our emotions and simply become caught up in their turmoil and our reaction, they become our emotional afflictions. The delusional nature of our mind and its inclination to fantasize and project from our emotional states then lead us to become even more bound by their power, without any way out. Our emotions really do become a problem rather than a resource. They become destructive emotions.

I am aware that within the Western Buddhist world there is some confusion around emotions. What I began to see in my own bridging of Buddhist and Western psychological views is that understanding how to work with emotions is not as straightforward as I thought earlier in my life as a Buddhist. As I indicated earlier, I became involved in Buddhism partly to resolve some of my emotional problems, and it has been an interesting journey of discovery. The realization gradually dawned that it is not my emotions that are the problem but how I am in relation to them. I think I always knew this, but it was, on occasion, difficult to negotiate the territory when I sometimes received such a strong teaching that emotions are the problem.

As we transform and open our relationship to the process of the emotions, they do not necessarily go away. They may diminish in intensity, they may flow through with greater ease and naturalness, they may simply form the rich and colorful background of the energy of our vitality. From a Mahamudra perspective, they are the fluid play of the energy of the mind, like the play of light in the aurora borealis of the northern night sky. I personally do not think I would want them to disappear into a sterile place of detached dissociation. Within the natural felt quality of the emotions is a wisdom that emerges as we are able to remain clear and spacious around them. In some Buddhist traditions, particularly the tantric tradition, it is the underlying energy of the emotions that forms the felt basis of much of our spiritual life. This is the nature of our emotional or energy body. In the tantric tradition, and in particular the practice of Mahamudra, the emotions are seen as the basis of particular dimensions of wisdom once their energy is liberated and transformed.

II

personifying
the emotions

A S WE LOOK AT THE transformation of our emotional
life, I wish to bring together a number of different
approaches coming from both Jung's work and the tantric
tradition. Something that I have found interesting in Jung's
exploration of our psychological life is that he appeared to
give less attention specifically to our emotions as such than
to what he called the complexes of the unconscious. He recognized that our emotions seldom arise in isolation and that
they are often clustered together around some central trauma
or experience that gives a kind of focus. He saw that for us to
begin to deal with this internal world of clusters of emotions,
we must first become conscious of its presence. Without this
conscious awareness, it remains within the unconscious as aspects of what he called the shadow.

It was Freud and then Jung who particularly used the notion of a threshold between consciousness and the unconscious. While this is not really an aspect of Buddhist thinking, it has nevertheless become central to Western understanding of the psyche. Both Freud and Jung saw the ego as a focus of attention sitting on that threshold, and its function is in part to filter and focus what comes through from the unconscious into consciousness. What is noticeably difficult for us in relation to the unconscious is that the contents of the unconscious, as Jung saw them, can erupt to the surface and potentially take over the ego. As the ego becomes taken over by the unconscious, we may feel we are literally drowning in the power of our emotional life.

Jung defined the complexes of the unconscious as "psychic entities that have escaped from the control of consciousness and split off from it, to lead a separate existence in the dark space of the psyche, whence they may at any time hinder or help conscious performance."[1] The complexes could be seen as collections of emotional charge and emotional habits that often tend to constellate around a particular central disposition. The closest we might come to understanding these in the context of Buddhist language is to recognize them as collections of karmic emotional habits or patterns with a central ego-grasping nature.

What Jung recognized with his idea of complexes was that these aspects of our psyche grow and shape themselves in such a way that they seem to have a life of their own within the sphere of the unconscious. They can then surge to the surface and completely dominate our sense of self. When someone pushes our buttons, so to speak, some unconscious complex

is called into life and comes to the surface, infusing our sense
of self with a strong emotional charge. When this happens we
become identified with the complex; it becomes all we are at
that instant. Roberto Assagioli, a contemporary of Jung's, described these complexes as subpersonalities and saw that they
did, indeed, literally take on a kind of personality of there
own.[2] When we begin to get to know these subpersonalities,
we may discover that we have within us a powerful needy
child, a dutiful good girl or boy, a tyrannical judge, a fanatical
controller, a wild man or woman desperate to get out, a sensitive creative soul, and so on. Assagioli saw that this family
of subpersonalities will often have relationships to each other
in ways that create an internal dysfunction. The stresses and
conflicts that we experience in ourselves can often be seen as
the conflicts between these inner characters. For example, the
inner judge may completely cripple our creative nature, or an
uptight inner moralist or disapproving parent may stifle our
playful sexual side.

Jung and Assagioli saw that because this inner dynamic is
largely unconscious, it can have a lot of power over us. If we
are able to become more conscious of these subpersonalities,
we begin to have a greater objectivity around them and can
disidentify from them. This term *disidentify* is very important
in understanding how we become conscious.

When we are taken over by one or another of our inner
complexes or subpersonalities, they dominate and color our
sense of self. At the heart of the collection of emotional habits
and patterns that make up the complex is a wounded sense
of self. When we are taken over by, say, the inner child, we
become completely identified with the emotional quality and

belief system of that child. This has the effect of coloring the world in a particular way, and yet we will be unable to recognize this process. When we are identified in this way, we have been pulled into the unconscious world and are blind to our reality.

This experience is very familiar in the therapeutic situation. A client I used to see who had an extremely wounded sense of self would become totally overwhelmed by the pain and despair of her childhood and could not easily find a way to come back to the reality of the present. She would get completely lost in this world and lose all contact with the room and with me. When she was in this space, I could see how cut off she was and how much pain she felt as she identified with this wounded inner child. It was a very slow and painful process to bring her gradually out of the identification so that she could begin to witness what was happening rather than be overwhelmed by it.

Disidentification from this kind of tendency takes time, as I have found in my own psychological journey. It is helped by an approach that Assagioli proposed of giving the complex a face and recognizing it as a subpersonality. It is then possible to see when we are suddenly dominated by the controller, the tyrannical child, the victim, or the like. We can, perhaps for the first time, name it to ourselves and see it emerge from the unconscious. We can still feel the power of its presence and the uncomfortable feelings it brings but not be completely lost in them.

Discovering this approach when I began to train as a psychotherapist was a revelation. I found myself seeing the multifaceted nature of my unconscious for the first time. I was reminded of Hermann Hesse's *Steppenwolf.* I also began to recognize more and more clearly the inner dynamic of conflicting needs and demands that ruled my life. And for the first time I was able to begin letting them dialogue with each other. This was another aspect of the disidentification process that brought understanding and some sense of resolution. Different aspects of our unconscious life have different needs and can struggle with each other as they fight for dominance. For example, another client had a strong disposition to be the controlling, competent one who could sort all problems and be seen as well and happy. She was so used to this way of being that she hardly saw it in herself. She came to me because she saw a side of herself that would come to the surface occasionally and be desperately needy and vulnerable. She feared this side because she thought it would cause her to lose control. The unconscious battle that went on was one where she, the controller, hated her inner child and its vulnerability. Only as we began to bring these two aspects of herself out in the open did we start to have a conversation between them and see what they wanted. What began to be clear was that the inner child felt constantly disregarded and abandoned by her other self. Her self-reliant controller was terrified of this need and wanted to shut her away. She could not let herself be vulnerable.

As we become more conscious of our subpersonalities, we begin to get a clearer picture of the dynamics of our emotional life. The gradual awareness this brings frees up our sense of self from the pull of this unconscious life. We are able to be more conscious because we are not taken over by the power of emotional patterns. This marks the beginning of a process that can then become more and more subtle as we are more able to witness our inner life.

When some people first come into the therapeutic setting, they may have almost no awareness of this inner life. They just *are* it, unconsciously and uncontrollably. This painful situation gradually becomes more workable as they are able to recognize the presence of strong and dominant emotional patterns. Working with subpersonalities is one way that we can do this. It can bring out into the open aspects of our inner family of emotional complexes and their interrelationships. We may all be familiar with the inner child, the critical judge, the strong carer, or the controlling organizer. When we look more deeply we may also discover some wilder aspects of ourselves that are less comfortable, like a wild and sexual woman, an aggressive bully, an aloof and arrogant adolescent, and so on.

It is within the world of our subpersonalities that we might begin to understand the presence of what have sometimes been called our inner demons. Whether we call them demons or subpersonalities, the intention is the same. We are waking up to their presence, and in doing so we begin to have a relationship for the first time. In working with a subpersonality, we can begin a dialogue where we discover how its life is, what its emotional wounding is, and what it may need to heal. In practice there are a number of ways we can do this that can be used both in the therapeutic setting between the therapist and the client and on our own in meditation.

One approach to this process is to begin by placing your awareness on some aspect of your emotional life that emerges in certain life situations. If there is some current difficulty that arises and causes you to respond in a particular way, place your attention on these feelings to allow time to deepen into them. You might ask yourself, if you were to give these feelings a personality, what it would be like. Find an image for it and then hold that image in your awareness to begin to get to know it more. An example of this arose with someone I once saw where he experienced a constant strong feeling of being harshly criticized. When he felt this, it was located around the upper part of his body, particularly in the shoulders. I suggested he feel into this experience and then gradually give the feelings a face and personality, as if it was someone living on his shoulders. He saw an ugly male figure that reminded him of a dwarf or goblin. I suggested he gradually bring this figure into the space before him and he began to speak with it.

When this kind of image arises you can begin to feel into the various emotions that constellate around the subpersonality, filling out your sense of its emotional life. As in the example above, it is extremely helpful to separate from the subpersonality and place it before you. You may then start to ask it some very simple questions. You might, for example, ask what has happened that has caused it to become the way it is. What is its story? You may feel into the particular emotional tone of the subpersonality and then ask what it needs. As you do this, you begin to gain a deeper sense of how it lives within you. You may also discover what its intention is in how it relates to you as the self. What does it want of you?

This approach can also be used to investigate the nature of physical symptoms such as pain and tension in parts of the body or even the discomfort of illnesses.[3] By placing our attention in the area of pain or tension, we can begin to expand an awareness of the sensations and feelings in that area. In a therapeutic context, it would then be natural for a therapist simply to ask the question: Do you have an image for what this is like? This can easily be turned toward personifying the personality of the pain or tension and then working with it as a subpersonality. In this way we may gradually bring to the surface some of the underlying emotions that lie beneath or within the pain, tension, or illness. Following the image in the way I have described before can then enable us to discover what it needs and how we might respond to that need.

Another approach that has been used in the context of transpersonal psychology for many years is an exercise that brings into awareness what we might call the family of subpersonalities. Through a process of guided imagery, a collection of subpersonalities is brought out and placed in a circle. This is sometimes done by imagining a house within which the subpersonalities dwell. They are then gradually brought out of the house until one senses that they are all present. Once they are gathered, it is possible to begin to see how they relate to each other. It becomes clearer which ones are in a positive relationship with each other and which are antagonistic or destructive. At this point one can also open some kind of dialogue between them that can enable the beginning of a healthier inner dynamic.

An example of this family of characters is depicted in the film *A Fish Called Wanda* cowritten by the actor John Cleese. Apparently Cleese attended a workshop in London at the Centre for Transpersonal Psychology, where he was taken through an exercise of the type I have just described, bringing out various subpersonalities. Following this exercise he wrote the characters into the film, creating a wonderfully comical

tale of their relationships. When we consider our subpersonalities in this way, it is easy to see how the characters in a play
or a story can depict the dynamics of someone's inner life.

Bringing some disturbing emotional experience before
us and opening up a dialogue with a personified image can
enable a much more conscious, accepting, and compassionate
relationship to something that has perhaps been disturbing
us for years. As we ask what this part of our psyche needs
from us, we might consider the approach that the author and
Western Buddhist teacher Tsultrim Allione uses of actually
"feeding the demon" out of a sense of compassion. She has
drawn from an old Tibetan tradition of *chöd,* where we make
an offering of our body to the demons in order to nourish and
transform them.⁴

If we begin to dialogue with our subpersonalities, we will
discover that they start to change. This dialogue can begin to
reveal the innate quality within a subpersonality that is positive and useful to us in our life. The inner persecuting critic
may become a valued guide to help us discover what is beneficial. The inner child who has felt lost and abandoned may
become peaceful and content for the first time. The wounded
and crippled creative side of ourselves may begin to feel able to
risk being creative and expressing itself.

Jung once said, "The gods have become our diseases,"⁵ and
one way we could interpret this is to recognize that within
the disturbed, sometimes crippled or even demonic aspects of
our unconscious life is the potential for extraordinary health.
The energy bound up in our unconscious subpersonalities is
not inherently bad or unhealthy. It simply needs to be brought
into a better, more-conscious relationship. As we care for

and look after these subpersonalities, they become resources throughout our life.

Many of our emotional patterns personified through subpersonalities are not far from conscious awareness, and we often know them only too well even if we haven't given them a face and worked with them in this way. There are also, however, deeper, darker, less known facets of our unconscious life that are aspects of what Jung described as our shadow, but these are often not so accessible to the process we have just been looking at. We require a subtly different approach to their awakening.

encountering
the shadow

No EXPLORATION INTO THE theme of feeling and
emotion is complete without considering the nature of
what Jung named the shadow. We may become increasingly
conscious of our feeling life by deepening our relationship to
the body and subtler levels of awareness, but there is an aspect of our nature that will still elude us. Even working with
subpersonalities does not necessarily bring this to the surface. Our shadow is by definition unconscious. It has become
buried in the unconscious of necessity as we've grown up because it is the unacceptable side of our nature. We gradually
learn that certain aspects of our emotional and instinctual
nature are not really accepted by family, friends, and the pre-
vailing culture, and consequently they become buried in the

unconscious. There they live on in the dark and actually gain strength in our denial and repression. Unfortunately, they do not simply go away. They remain buried until some circumstance evokes their presence and power from the underworld. It is the emergence of the shadow in its full force that can be the most disturbing, frightening, and often shameful or embarrassing experience. It is important to recognize, however, that there is much more to the shadow than just repressed emotion and erupting emotional affect.

Of course, we may think that the shadow, because it is seen as the darker side of our nature, is bad and negative. It is indeed held in the dark, but this does not imply it is inherently bad. Because it has been held in the dark, it has tended to become distorted and untamed by conscious integration. It is often the wild, undeveloped side of our nature, however, that is usually antithetical to moral prescriptions in a spiritual context. The danger of making what is natural, spontaneous, and expressive unacceptable in a spiritually correct environment is that it will become buried in the shadow.

Possibly the most familiar aspects of our nature that become buried in this way are our aggression, power, and sexuality, but we can also find many subtler permutations of our more-instinctual side hiding in the dark. It may be that some of the vitality that we need in our life is buried in the shadow and has therefore become inaccessible to us. The shadow may contain aspects of our creativity and abilities that we have repressed, often through fear and unacceptability. Someone who suffers deep feelings of doubt and lack of confidence can often have abilities buried in the shadow that are desperate to emerge. Some familiar examples of suppressed aspects of our nature are creative abilities, expressions of power and assertiveness, spontaneity and playfulness, and even sexuality.

There are two ways that our shadow first becomes apparent to us. One is when it surges through from the unconscious and upsets our ego's normal control over our behavior. It is the kind of thing that may come out if we drink too much, because our normal monitoring control weakens. It may come out in times of heated arguments, when we hear ourselves say things that shock even us. It may manifest in circumstances like driving our car when our normal sense of control gives way to outbursts of rage at other drivers. The shadow can also emerge when we are under great stress. Someone who is normally considerate of others may suddenly become extremely selfish and greedy.

The other way in which we get to know the shadow is through our projections. It was clear to Jung that our shadow is very often projected onto those around us in the form of strong fears, prejudices, and judgments. Our shadow appears to manifest in those we feel jealousy or repulsion toward and who seem to push our buttons or irritate us. The problem is that we fail to recognize that we have projected something of ourselves onto another.

We see this manifesting in many different ways both individually and collectively in our culture. It was noticeable in the prejudices between the Western and Soviet worlds during the Cold War. It was present in the hatred expressed during the peak of the Protestant-Catholic conflicts in Ireland, and it is there in the background of the prejudices that arise in relation to the Islamic world. When the shadow emerges, it is very irrational and full of emotional affect.

The danger is that we can take it very seriously and believe what we think we see. Jung found in his exploration of the shadow that the brighter, more positive, and good conscious life becomes, the darker our shadow also becomes. We do not get awakened, he said, by becoming light and bright but by integrating the shadow. This means that when we consider our spiritual life, it is important that the shadow be gradually brought into awareness; otherwise our spirituality just becomes a perpetuation of the split between what we feel is light, good, and acceptable and what is unacceptable, dark, or "evil." The perennial struggle between good and evil in various religions does not resolve the shadow, it merely drives it deeper into the unconscious. There it potentially becomes demonic. It is interesting to note that in Buddhism the dichotomy is between ignorance and wisdom, between not-seeing and seeing, rather than good and evil. When we then consider the shadow, the problem is not whether it is good or bad but whether we are conscious or unconscious of its presence.

When we come to the point of recognizing the need to reawaken our relationship to the shadow, we will, as Jung said, need a strong container that can hold the dark god as it is released from the underworld. When the shadow reemerges, it brings with it a huge amount of powerful energy and, often, strong emotion. When the shadow emerges, it is potent, partly because it has been held in a repressed state and partly because its nature is intrinsically bound up with our innate power and vitality. This can be overwhelming unless it is held skillfully.

Skillful holding means two things: one is that we need to be willing to take responsibility for what we have arising within us; the other is that we need to be aware that it will affect others and that we must not let it harm others. Often we fear that when the shadow reemerges it will be dangerous and harm others. This can make us feel that we are too much or that others will not cope with it. In many ways this may be true. The shadow may be dangerous, especially if it is full of anger and rage. This means that acting it out and harming others are as unhelpful as suppressing it has become. Neither of these transforms its nature. Transforming the shadow often requires some kind of alchemical vessel, some sort of channel for the energy that arises. This may be therapeutic, it may be a very practical channel of some activity, or it could be a med-itation retreat.

As I've worked in the context of meditation retreats, it has been very clear that the shadow can begin to emerge as the heat of the process increases. When my wife, Anna, and I work together, we often need to hold people pyschologically through a process of reawakening the shadow. We have found that retreat can offer a safe context where the forces of the shadow can begin to reawaken and be held and integrated. Retreat is in this sense a very powerful alchemical vessel. Sometimes transformation then occurs specifically through the process of meditation, where the energy of the shadow is released and channeled internally. At other times it is through the process of movement, where the strong energy of emotions such as anger can be wrestled with and integrated through the body. This is something we will look at in chapter 14.

An example of this reemergence of the shadow was very apparent in a client who was given a very clear message throughout much of her childhood that her sexuality was not acceptable. As she grew into womanhood, her sense of herself as a woman required that the sexual side of her nature be kept hidden because it was shameful. It was in the process of many years of therapy and her relationship to a particular tantric-deity practice that her natural sexual nature began to reawaken. At first this was very disturbing because it brought so much shame and the fear that she was going to be judged and condemned by others. Finding people who supported her in this journey and valued her as she opened up to her sexuality provided a safe context in which to release this shadowy side of her nature. She began to feel that her sexuality was not shameful or bad, just very powerful. It was wonderful to see that she was gradually able to find a natural expression of this side of herself and that it could come out of the shadows and manifest in her life.

Whatever method we use to awaken and integrate the shadow, it is not a comfortable process and requires the willingness to stay with it and gradually allow the shadow space to be part of us. This needs a compassionate quality of nonjudgment that lets it be what it is rather than our feeling that it is wrong and that we are being bad for feeling what we feel. Aggression, power, and sexual desire are potent forces, and we are so often reluctant to let them come through, and yet this is sometimes what we need to do to transform and integrate. On one level they are just powerful energy, and if we can be open to it and begin to embody it consciously, we will discover an extraordinary resource in ourselves.

It is not uncommon to find that our relationship to our power is so poor that its only outlet is anger. Once it is brought back from the shadow, we may for the first time feel we can actually embody our sense of power without its becoming distorted into anger. We may equally find with sexuality that we are able to live comfortably within our body as a sexual and awake person without fear and without feeling it is uncontained or wrong. We may also begin to feel, for the first time, that we can truly be who we are.

The shadow contains vitality in us that will be a wonderful resource once we begin to integrate it into our experience. It is the raw essence of our awakening and is overlooked at our cost. It may bring with it strong emotional experiences as it comes awake, but with skill and a willingness to embark on the journey, we will benefit hugely from its awakening and transformation. Possibly the most powerful way this happens is in a process of embodiment that we will explore in relation to movement.

13

the energy body

IN THE BUDDHIST TANTRIC tradition, the approach to working with the emotions and the shadow introduces another way of being with our experience. Emphasis is taken away from the emotions as such by seeing the underlying energetic process as more important. The energy body is also sometimes known as the emotional body because it is understood to be at the very heart of our emotional life. This energy body is a very real experience even though we still have no way of scientifically measuring it. In the East, this subtle body is known as the body of *prana* (Skt.) in the world of Indian yoga, *lung* in the world of Tibetan Buddhism, and *qi* or *chi* in Chinese medicine. As I have suggested in *The Psychology of Buddhist Tantra,* Jung's notion of spirit as a "subtle, volatile, active and vivifying essence" is perhaps the closest equivalent we might find in the West.[1] The terms *lung* and *prana* have increasingly been translated as "energy wind" as they apply to the experience in both meditation and yoga.

Within the tantric tradition it is recognized that the essential nature of the emotions is energy wind. This vitality underlies and pervades all of our emotional and feeling experiences, yet it is only recognized as such once we begin to orient our awareness to its nature. I alluded to this in chapter 3 when I referred to the energy or vitality of our basic aliveness. When we meditate with increasingly still awareness in the subtlety of our feelings, we can start to recognize this essential vitality of the energy winds.

The way in which the energy winds underlie the emotions is very simple. When we experience strong emotional disturbances and are very agitated, this is a reflection of the agitation and imbalance of the energy winds. When we experience subtler feelings, the energy winds are in a more-peaceful, balanced, less-agitated state. This means that the stronger emotions such as anger, jealousy, and desire arise from highly activated energy winds, whereas feelings such as love and compassion arise from calmer, gentler energy winds.

Although I am saying the emotions arise from these energy winds, in fact we can say that these two are the same process viewed from different perspectives. When the energy winds are agitated, this is manifested in the various emotions we are experiencing in our awareness. From a tantric point of view, every aspect of our mind is underpinned by energy wind. The mind or consciousness is intimately connected to energy wind, from its most subtle aspect of clear-light mind to the gross manifestations of a disturbed and agitated mind. When the mind is agitated and disturbed by worries and fears, equally, the energy winds are stimulated as a felt affect. They are inseparable, and the metaphor that is often used to illustrate this is of a horse and its rider. There is a familiar image in the Tibetan world of what is called *lungta,* or wind horse (fig. 5), where a flaming jewel is riding on the back of a horse, which represents the mind riding the energy winds. When the wind horse is wild and bucking, the mind is thrown around; when the wind horse is calm and steady, the mind can also be so.

What this metaphor leads to is the recognition that any state of mind or emotion has an energetic component; they are inseparable. Furthermore, the energy-wind process is also intimately connected to our physical body; in fact, we can say that it pervades our body. This means that whether we are aware of it or not, there is a constant presence of the energetic process within the body on relatively subtle levels. It also means that if we have a tendency to split off from feelings or to suppress emotions in an attempt to avoid or subdue them, their underlying energy does not go away but buries itself in the body and becomes the basis of all manner of disturbances and potential illness.

This understanding of the energetic process within our emotional and feeling life is increasingly familiar to the West and offers a way of working with our emotional life that can be very beneficial. It also gives us a way of understanding the mind-body-emotion relationship that is an important part of psychological and physical health. The energy body is, from an Eastern point of view, the bridge between emotional and physical processes. The implications of this are very important.

What we do to our body, what we feed it, and the way we treat it will, through the vehicle of the energy winds, affect our emotional life. The way we deal with our emotional life, through the vehicle of the energy winds, will have its impact upon the body and its health.

From a tantric point of view, if we wish to work with our emotional life, we must begin to address its energetic nature. When we wake up buried emotions held in the body, we release the energy that is bound up with them. This may be very painful to experience; it may equally be very liberating or healing. Once the energy winds are healed in this way, they begin to manifest in their innate quality, which brings great inner satisfaction, peace, and happiness.

In the tantric tradition, it is this emphasis on working with the energetic processes that is at the heart of practices of meditation as well as certain physical exercises. The aim of these practices is not to get rid of our feeling life; rather, it is to release and transform its underlying energy. Working with the energy winds can be very liberating. It can particularly mean that we begin to be able to watch emotional processes pass through us without becoming so caught up in their psychological content. If, for example, I experience a strong emotion such as fear and feel it passing through me as an experience of energy, I can let it pass without becoming entangled in the potential projections and fantasies that arise with fear. It is just an energetic process moving through me. The same applies to strong feelings of anger, grief, desire, jealousy, and so on. In the tantric tradition, the energy of these feelings is the raw ingredient of our awakening. Once this raw vitality is freed to move through, its nature changes as it becomes transformed into an essential energy that is not bound by emotional affect but is felt very deeply and subtly. In the practice of tantra, the energy of the emotions once liberated in this way becomes a blissful wisdom.

When we start to work with the energetic process that underlies our feeling life, our relationship to the body is paramount. If we are out of relationship to the body, we will have a poor capacity to be with both our feelings and the energy winds that underlie them. Once we restore this relationship, however, our innate vitality begins to return in a very powerful way, freeing the energy that has been blocked and defiled, bringing greater capacity for health and a happier and more comfortable sense of self.

Some of us can experience a kind of low-grade discomfort with ourselves and within our body. This may manifest as a subtle depressive quality or a sense of listlessness and lack of positivity in our life. We may seldom experience genuine pleasure and happiness that are not dependent on some kind of stimulation through the senses. This can make us continually restless and dissatisfied, and the search for external satisfaction is potentially endless. When we begin to refine and develop the energy-wind body, we start to free ourselves from a kind of energetic toxicity and stagnation that has accumulated throughout our life. This can mean that for the first time, we begin to experience a genuine sense of inner satisfaction and ease. As this grows, real, lasting happiness becomes possible not because of some external stimulation but as a deeply felt experience in our vitality. We all have this potential within our energy body, but it will not arise without our beginning to clear what pollutes it. For this reason, in the tantric tradition in particular, there is a great emphasis on what is considered to be a healing and purification of the energy-wind body. As we purify and heal the energy body and release trauma held there, the innate potential of our vitality naturally emerges. We may then start to experience what is seen as the natural bliss at the core of our being. This profound felt quality is the nature of our mind in its most refined and natural state as a union of blissful energy and clarity.

It is within the practice of tantra that emphasis is placed upon practices that help to heal and purify the energy winds. Some of these are complicated visualizations and mantra practices that refine and cleanse the energy winds; others are active practices that work specifically through the body. It is through working with the body in movement that some of the most powerful transformation can occur.

FIG. 5. *Wind horse (author's rendition)*.

14

moving through the body

Anna Murray Preece

To this point you have been looking at the transformation of your feeling and emotional life and its underlying energy winds. It is helpful to recognize that as feelings arise, they also need to be "digested" or moved through the body in order to be fully released. When my oldest son was a baby, he had an incredible way of expressing joy and excitement. His body would vibrate, and with his arms stuck out in front of him, he would emit an excited gurgle. It seemed to me to be a mixture of laughter, pure satisfaction, and what one might call "feeling the force." It was wonderful to witness total joy without inhibition, his capacity to allow energy simply to move and flow through him. Nowadays, of course, he is a cool teenager with a lot of control over his emotions.

This direct link between feelings and the body becomes very apparent when you look at any young and healthy child. We can see this in the immediate response of thwarted toddlers, stamping their feet or lying on the ground kicking and screaming to express how they feel. It is natural to cry when upset or to want to hide when frightened. Gaining a sense of control over emotions is part of growing up; however, this is a mixed blessing, and often a lot can be lost in the process. Of course we need to know boundaries and what is appropriate, but the danger is that we lose the capacity to allow feelings to move and release through the body. For many of us, this is suppression in a quest to appear normal; for others it can be a frozen response to severe trauma. It is also a reflection of the lack of support and general understanding in our society of the need to allow emotions their natural place. There is a lot of fear around the expression of strong feelings, especially grief and anger. Even joy is often expressed only after a large dose of alcohol. As a result, many people have become so tight and held in their body that it can be devastating to health and general well-being.

Connecting with emotions through bodywork and movement can begin to reestablish the physiological links between the emotions and the body. How one might work with this varies with each individual, depending upon the person's capacity to tolerate being in connection with her or his body and feelings. At one end of the spectrum, someone who has been very traumatized may well have needed to find ways to dissociate totally from the body and its sensations. At the other end, one might encounter an emotionally robust individual who is sensitive enough to be in contact with feelings and sensations as they arise. Working with emotions through movement can support a process that opens to and allows what is there in any moment so that the energy held can find its natural expression. In doing this it is not uncommon that uncomfortable feelings arise, and so it is important that the process is held by the therapist with care and compassion. Part of this care is to recognize the limits of each individual. This means that when feelings arise that are hard to tolerate it is counterproductive to push a person to stay with them. Learning how to tolerate the intolerable is nevertheless a useful part of the healing process. As a person becomes stronger in themselves they will be more able to bear emotions they hitherto could not. Allowing this process to evolve naturally is essential in holding a safe space that supports change rather than entrenching old patterns.

There are many ways of working with emotions through movement. My own preference over many years is now to work with Rhythmic Healing, a form of spontaneous, nonstylized movement that facilitates the embodiment of what is arising moment to moment. One of the core principles of Rhythmic Healing is to support a sense of trust in one's own rhythm. Through this there is a growth of the capacity to be with oneself and one's body energy without a need to push or hold back. This brings us back to our core nature as well as connecting us more deeply with the rhythm of the earth we live on. This supports the capacity to listen and open to the natural dynamic of energy in the body and allow its expression through movement and stillness. This can be done alone once a capacity to stay with a process has been developed. However, it is possible to go much deeper when there is someone present who is experienced in holding the process with a quality of love, care, and compassion.

In order to reestablish or deepen our capacity for this listening, it is helpful to be able to develop mindful awareness of sensation and feeling in the body, a capacity to "receive one-self." It is then possible to begin to open to the natural impulses for movement, whether they are very gentle and subtle or more physically expressive. This is a natural process, as we are moving all the time in response to our environment. Our bodies are highly tuned in this way, both as a survival instinct and as a necessity in our daily lives. With practice we can become more present and aware of how we respond and how our body moves in relationship to our internal world as well as what is outside.

As mentioned above, an essential ingredient of this approach to movement is that we begin to connect with our own rhythm and timing. If we allow ourselves to feel when and how we want to move, a process can awaken that will align us very deeply. Much of life these days is spent being out of relationship both to the natural rhythm within ourself and to the rhythms of nature and the earth. Learning to sense what needs to move and when encourages a capacity to honor an intimate relationship with ourself.

This intimate relationship is not so different from any other intimate relationship, in that it is fed by feelings of pleasure and satisfaction. Building a relationship with ourself that allows a sense of nourishment and satisfaction enables a capacity to know when our energy is flowing in a healthy direction. This is a natural and innate gift we all have, but in the highly structured world in which we live, it is often driven out of us or suppressed from an early age. For example, as children we may not have been allowed to stop eating even when we were full because we were required to eat all that was on our plate. We may have been made to sit still in class even though energy was coursing through our body so that we wanted to move and express ourselves physically. Many of us have been taught to ignore what satisfies and nourishes. Rebuilding this capacity to feel for and follow what is satisfying may not always be easy, but it is very profound. It brings a gift of alignment with ourselves that draws on a natural capacity that, once reawoken, can have a huge effect on how we live our lives. Even when we touch difficult emotions, if we are working with them in a way that is potentially transformative, we will often experience a sense of rightness or satisfaction that has to do with connecting with a healthy flow of energy. This can be felt in the sense of relief when dammed-up tears can at last flow in the wake of a great grief, in the satisfaction of clenching our muscles and growling when feeling frustrated, or stamping our foot when we feel angry.

An important aspect of working in this way is developing the capacity to be in touch with the felt sense. It gives us the ability to sit with ourselves, be in touch with our body, and witness our emotions as they arise. Because we are then less identified with emotions, there is greater spaciousness, making it easier to allow the process to unfold. This can enable us to get underneath habitual movement patterns. These patterns are there for a good reason. They are a protection from being in touch with emotions and feelings that have remained unresolved, usually because they were too much to tolerate at the time they originally arose. As such, these habits are a holding pattern. They are in place to enable life to carry on through difficult times, but ideally they do not stay forever. They make it possible to live with what is unresolved until we enter an environment that is safe enough to begin to open up to what is held and allow it to be released through the body.

A simple example of this is how tension in the shoulders can hold feelings that have been given little space to be expressed.

Connecting to these feelings through body awareness and movement can enable a dynamic process of deep unraveling in the body and the whole being. As the capacity to be with this process increases, we will discover the ability to allow emotion to be released and transformed. When the emotional and physical connection becomes stronger, there can be a natural sense of what is needed, be it a gentle shake of the arm or a more vigorous movement. The potential here is for the energy to arise and be expressed in a way that naturally results in an embodied release that is both satisfying and a true letting go.

One of the beauties of connecting to the body through movement is that it is not necessary to understand what is happening intellectually, and in fact, it is often beneficial to drop beneath the need to understand the process. In letting go into what is happening, the body can begin to allow a healing process to occur spontaneously. Getting involved cognitively in the story is not necessary, although, of course, sometimes it will feel helpful. Often the process goes beneath what is conscious and takes us into what has hitherto been unknown. One client described how this touched her in our sessions: "I arrived feeling distracted and deeply tired. I sorely needed the opportunity to come back into relationship with my body. Although I noticed the usual tendency for my mind to take charge and make my movements graceful or purposeful, I gradually allowed myself to settle and be moved by my body in an instinctual way. Soon my thoughts were taking more of a backseat."

With those who are new to using movement as a tool for healing, it often helps to give a more specific focus, such as connecting to a particular part of the body. This could be an aspect of the body, such as the muscles or skin, or a particular part, such as the spine or feet. Focusing in this way can help to ground the process and gives many people a sense of security and structure from which to work. In observing a person moving, it often becomes clear to me where energy is held or where there is a particular strength. Focusing on or exploring this area of the body will often be helpful. Our body holds so much information that connecting to any part will be a rich experience. I have also found specific exercises such as these to be a good way to warm up a group or an individual to his or her sense of connection to the body. As people become more in touch with the body and its responses, they will also become more attuned to what works for them as a focus. For example, a client began to notice that her thighs were a place of strength and stability, and so putting her attention on them helped her to be more grounded and in touch with herself. Becoming aware in this way opens up a resource that can be taken into daily life and can be very empowering.

Facilitating a larger group often requires a more generalized approach and more specific guidelines. For example, during a recent retreat there were a number of people in the group, notably most of the men, whose movements I noticed had a particularly linear quality. I suggested that they explore moving in a more circular fashion. This brought about some amusement but also a sense of new ways of perceiving themselves in relation to their inner processes and what was around them. It gave them a means to open to a different aspect of themselves that had not been so apparent before. It was wonderful to see them twirling around the room with a sense of liberation in their energy.

Working with emotions through movement can result in very dynamic physical expression or a deep sense of stillness. It can also facilitate a connection with subtler movements of feeling and energy. When the space is held safely, it can offer the possibility of healing deep trauma. A client described a process of "re-membering" her body as she became reacquainted with herself through loving touch, healing the brusque, offhand way that she had been treated and touched as a child. Another client I have been working with has been through a profound process of allowing herself her own rhythm. Here it becomes clear that not *having* to move is the important thing, and what is needed is to be allowed the space to let movement come in its own time. This client says, "After years of working on my deep patterning of 'doing' to get loved and accepted, I am now finally getting the message into my bones and flesh to allow what I long for: just to be there with and for myself while being in the presence of others. Not only is it okay to do nothing and just be, but that doing nothing is powerfully transformational."

I am always inspired to hear when someone begins to find how she or he can use movement as a resource in daily life. Another person I work with described how she deals with waking in the night with anxiety. "Basically, I wriggle around, but in a slow way, flexing, stretching, and generally moving all of my body in a way that feels very relaxing and comforting. Then I stop moving and relax completely and monitor how the anxiety feels. Mostly, it has dissipated. If not, then I repeat the movement until I feel completely relaxed and able to fall back into sleep again."

There are two dimensions to this work that I would like to describe. One I will call the technical and the other the transpersonal or "spiritual." When I first started working with people I was more oriented toward using methods and techniques that enabled a deepening connection and experience of the body. This echoed my own positive experience of relearning to connect with myself in this way. Through my own journey I was able to enjoy my relationship with my body and find expression, healing, clarity, and inspiration. My aim was to feel more "embodied," to be able to stay more in touch with myself as I moved through the world. Being in touch with my own processes as they arose, I discovered, also enhanced my ability to be in touch with what was around me and increased my sensitivity to others.

Over the years of working with movement in relation to emotions, what has become more and more clear to me is the relationship between the body and what we might call spirit, or the transpersonal. There is a significant value in the connection between the grounding quality of relating to the body through sensation and feeling, and opening to something beyond our secular understanding. It is of course the case that every spiritual path has its body aspect, be it yoga, tai chi, or any other form. What is not so obvious in these paths, however, is how to incorporate and work with emotional states in a way that our Western psyche can relate to. I have found the degree of disconnection to the body that many people experience benefits from this more direct approach. What is vital, however, is that the spirit is not left out. More than that, the process of directly opening to spirit both quickens and enhances the process. This has been enhanced for me through the training I received in Rhythmic Healing[1] and has evolved through the work I have done since with individuals.

I feel that the depth that my clients now reach in sessions, as in the examples I have given above, is very much supported by this. Connecting in this way enables a greater capacity to open my heart and be present with compassion. I feel this is the result of allowing myself to ask for and receive support. What might be happening or causing this is beyond my ordinary understanding, but what I feel is that placing myself in relationship to a spiritual presence allows me to sit in a truer place. It encourages a sense of humility that knows the healing is not from me but from something beyond. It reminds me of my small place in the world, allowing me to be a conduit for energy rather than just a facilitator. Bodywork and movement can be effective without this relationship; however, my experience of this deeper connection is that very remarkable and beautiful shifts can be made.

Anna Murray Preece has worked as a movement therapist with individuals and groups for many years. She originally trained with Sandra Reeve as a Move into Life facilitator, and she studied extensively with Suprapto Suryadarmo and other teachers of movement. More recently she trained in Rhythmic Healing, a dynamic movement process developed by the late Ruth Noble. This now forms the heart of Anna's work. Rhythmic Healing is a subtle style of therapeutic movement that sits well alongside the practice of meditation. Anna and I have led many retreats together creating a rhythm of meditation and movement as a way of practice. During these retreats people consistently say how deeply the movement process affects their capacity for meditation, enabling a deepening of their receptiveness to themselves and facilitating the natural liberation and embodiment of emotional process. This work also helps to create a bridge between the inner process of meditation and how this is brought into daily life. For this reason Anna's experience is an invaluable addition to this book.

wisdom
energy

15

the nature
of passion

IN MY EARLY YEARS AS A Buddhist practitioner, I felt I
needed to hide the more passionate side of myself so as to
be a peaceful, wholesome, spiritually correct practitioner. I've
never been sure how I got this idea, although it tended to be
implicit in many of the teachings I received: that I needed to
subdue my mind and its passionate side. As a result I found
myself living in a somewhat repressive regime that was partly
of my own making but also part of the collective culture. Perhaps this also had some basis in the Protestant culture within
which I grew up, which had a somewhat puritanical edge to
it that did not readily welcome the expression of passion. In
spite of this, I would often feel passionately about some of the
things I did or valued, and I could feel this about my spiritual

life as well. I have often wondered how it would have been if I had grown up in a Latin country like Italy or Spain, and I was often very at home with some of my Latin peers in the Buddhist world who also seemed to have a strong sense of passion. I recall Lama Yeshe once joking that he could see our cultural differences and that one day there would be German Buddhism, English Buddhism, and Italian Buddhism.

The view I was learning—that the body, speech, and mind had to be tamed, subdued, and restrained for me to be a "good Buddhist"—in many ways reinforced my Protestant puritanical background. Unwittingly, I was becoming a puritanical Buddhist. Yet running beneath this restraint was a side of my nature that could feel passionately about aspects of my life, things I believed in or was inspired by. My passion motivated me to engage with my study and practice of the dharma, and I was very aware that my engagement was less intellectual and academic than it was something I felt passionate about. Intuitively, I felt that my passion was connected to my innate vitality rather than just being delusion or emotional affect. It seemed to come through my need to be creative and express myself. This led me to a fundamental dilemma. Is my passionate side a problem, or is it fundamental to my energy for life?

As my practice deepened and I found myself increasingly engaged in the tantric tradition, the passionate side of my nature began to feel some resonance and inclusion. Within the world of tantra practice is a small group of deities associated with the transformation of desire and passion into a blissful wisdom. These deities include Chakrasamvara, Hevajra, Vajrayogini, and Vajravarahi, all of whom are seen as manifestations of our innate Buddha nature, specifically embodying the transformation of passion and desire. Indeed, in the Chakrasamvara tantra it says quite specifically that in times when desire and passion are strong, the deities' power is increasingly effective. This, one might think, is so that the deities have a greater capacity to subdue and overcome desire. To the contrary, however, these deities do not subdue the passion of desire; they channel it and give it an extraordinary vehicle for transformation and expression.

Now I started to feel that my passion had a place. With this channel of awakening, my innate nature had a home that did not say it was bad or wrong but, rather, that it was the very juice of my enlightened nature. These tantras were there to harness the vitality of our passion and refine and transform it into an extremely potent cocktail of blissful wisdom.

Of course, passion is undoubtedly problematic in that it can become excessive and overwhelming or out of control. It will inevitably express itself through our sexuality, and the energy of passion is closely linked to the nature of desire. However, perhaps we can say that it is not the energy or vitality of our passion that is the problem but our relationship to it. Perhaps we could begin to see passion as the vitality that comes through what we do and gives a quality of engagement and motivation to it. What this energy attaches itself to may be a problem, which is ultimately reflected in whether it leads to health and happiness or to something more destructive.

In *Preparing for Tantra* I give the example of a friend whose vitality was very strong and yet never found a natural channel within his Buddhist practice. As a result he would swing from periods of indulgence in sex and hard drugs that took him into a very destructive world to periods of repression and seemingly pure living. He tried to live a wholesome lifestyle that would be seen by his friends in the Buddhist world as exemplary of a "good Buddhist." I knew him well and was aware that the other side of his nature, full of passion and sexual energy, was being suppressed. It was on the event of his death from a drug overdose that the real conflict between these aspects of his nature came to light. Many of his Buddhist peers did not really know he had this other side and found it hard to reconcile this with their idealized view of him. His friends from Narcotics Anonymous were a little less naive regarding his struggle.[1]

This friend was someone who had a very passionate nature and no way to really transform it. He was not alone in this, and I feel sure that only when we can see the validity of this side of ourselves as an aspect of our spiritual life will we genuinely begin to find a way to transform it.

In my early years as a Buddhist, I was very unclear about how to relate to the sexual side to this vitality. I received mixed messages, some suggesting that sexuality was a source of confusion and suffering because it led to deluded behavior, that is, sex. Sexual misconduct was not just about having sex with the wrong person at the wrong time—it tended to be sexual contact, full stop. This did not sit easily with me, and I could see that it motivated many of my peers to become monks and nuns. They felt this would solve the problem, even though, ironically, it meant that some of them thought even more about sex.

Again, it is in the context of tantric practice that this side of our nature has some validity. Unfortunately, however, it is the sexual aspect that has become most distorted in the popular view of tantra in the West. People giving weekend courses on tantric sex promotes the idea that tantra is just a practice to heighten sexual experience, which, regrettably, denigrates the understanding of the term *tantra* itself. Even so, it is in the context of tantra that the vitality of our sexuality has a significant place in the process of transformation. It is this same vitality that lies at the heart of our passionate side, even though it is not always expressed sexually. I have always known that my need or perhaps drive to be creative has a strong relationship to my sexual energy. Psychologically, this is a well-known phenomenon, and Jung and Freud saw libido as a natural instinctual drive at the heart of our life vitality. Without this energy we would all be somewhat passive, lifeless souls. They recognized that when our natural libido is blocked or dammed up, it comes out in ways that are not healthy. Then it can also be the basis of physical and psychological illness.

There is a natural vitality to our nature that is an innate part of our life in the human body. One of the ways in which this vitality expresses itself is in the inspiration and passion to be creative. The transformation of our passion and vitality does not mean it will go away or become subdued and diminished. It means that we will be able to harness its power and potency in a truly awakened way. How we awaken and channel our passion is then very significant. Joseph Campbell used the expression "to follow one's bliss," implying that we should learn to listen to what deeply moves us in life. When we are passionate in being true to our journey through life, it will bring with it great joy and happiness. It will bring a deep sense of meaning and inspiration.

Passion is a vital power in our nature that can be at the heart of our awakening. I feel that in my own life I would not have gone into retreat with the intensity I did if I had not felt passionately about it. That gave me the energy and determination to continue and does to this day. I feel passionately about the tantric path and its extraordinary beauty and inspiration. I have always felt passionate about my work as a psychotherapist, and I feel increasingly passionate about bringing my tantric practice into relationship with elements and energies within the natural environment. We should not underestimate the value of our passion and the ways in which it can be harnessed and channeled. It is not just a mental phenomenon; it is an energetic experience that can run through whatever we do.

The question that arises is, how do we learn to relate to our passion in a healthy way? It is clear that too much passion in what we do can lead to fanaticism, fundamentalism, and potentially destructive compulsion. Too little passion and we may feel that our life is without meaning, dead, and uninspiring. The energy of passion comes from deep within our psyche and has a quality that can inflame and inspire us. It motivates and compels us to engage in what we do. If we consider the metaphor of fire, we see that it can be a mixed blessing. As an expression of our innate vitality, passion is perhaps without a moral compass: it is simply energy that could be directed toward what is beneficial or what is unwholesome. We have seen how destructive and aggressive fundamentalism can be when fired up. It is one of the most destructive expressions of our passion. Equally, the passion one man I know described in his desire to make his fortune drove him to an incredibly unhealthy extreme. He saw how there could be a manic side to this energy when it was not controlled skillfully. For him the path was to find a balance and integrity in his passionate nature.

There is an expression that comes from the Mexican shamans: "a sickness of the soul's calling." What this expression reflects is that when we are aligned with our natural spiritual calling, the energy of our passion will flow naturally. When we are out of alignment, it will manifest in all manner of sickness, both physically and psychologically. To allow our passion to be a natural and healthy aspect of our life is to see its alignment with what is meaningful and beneficial for us and others. When our passion is aligned with a positive, meaningful intention, it can be deeply fulfilling. Once we begin to feel this, we also need to recognize what can make this become unhealthy. Like a powerful wild horse, the energy needs to be gradually channeled and to some degree tamed. This taming does not imply we need to repress our passion but more that we must learn to ride it skillfully. Too much leads to a driven compulsion; too little and we can feel dead and uninspired.

What needs to be addressed in our passion is the degree to which the ego is involved. When the ego contracts and grasps at the power of our passion, it can become obsessive and compulsive. It becomes a force that can take us over and drive us, becoming destructive both to us and to others. The ego can be a vehicle for our passion as it aligns itself with something meaningful, or it can be taken over by passion and effectively become driven by it. The danger with our ego's involvement is that we can begin to push rather than respond. If our passion is allowed to flow without our ego's being so caught up in its intention, it can become a natural expression of our vitality, moving us creatively. The root of our vitality is based in the energy of our innate nature, our Buddha potential, or what Jung called the Self. When we align ourselves with this deeper level of intention, it becomes a source of tremendous vitality and inspiration for engaging with and accomplishing our life's goals. Then our passion becomes an energy that can be channeled for the welfare of others. The quality of intention known as *bodhichitta,* or the awakening mind, in Buddhism can bring with it some sense of this alignment of our passion. *Bodhichitta* is a heartfelt intention to dedicate our life to awaken for the welfare of others. If we align our natural sense of passion with this awakening heart mind, our passion becomes a potent motivating force in our life. It can inform much of what we do and provide a natural energy and vitality for embarking upon the journey of our life with joy and love. Of course, this passion will need to be balanced so that its heat does not burn too fiercely, but equally, it needs not to be extinguished by too much constraint and control. The fire of our passion is a natural expression of our nature if we can align it with a sense of what is true in our heart. It then becomes the core energy and inspiration of our awakening. It becomes what Lama Yeshe called our wisdom energy.

heart values

WHEN SOME OF MY Tibetan teachers first began to visit the West and teach Westerners, they were surprised or perhaps even shocked by something they experienced in us. When they described it in their own terms, they called it *soklung,* a damage or blockage of the primary energy wind within the heart chakra. What they recognized was that something about our way of life in the West was putting a kind of pressure in the heart that led to a subtle level of pain and depression of the energy there. One of the ways this manifests is in subtle yet deep insecurity, anxiety, and unhappiness.

If we translate this into Western psychological language, what we begin to understand is that there is something about the stresses and pressures we grow up with in the West that has a dramatic impact upon this very subtle energy in the heart. One of the most significant aspects of this is that we experience a much more accentuated sense of insecurity and alienation in the West because of the very nature of our culture and its expectations of us from a very early age. From early in our life we are more likely to experience separation from the mother and a far greater expectation that we be independent and self-reliant. We grow up into a world that then demands that we survive and become an individual in an extremely competitive environment, where the pressure to succeed is endemic. If we add to this a disintegration of supportive community and the dysfunctionality of the nuclear family, insecurity, anxiety, and fear become a root emotional drive.

Is it any wonder that this has an impact on the heart and on the energy of the heart? The consequence is that we experience a deep-rooted wounding to our sense of self, and thus our ego identity is built on shaky ground from the very beginning. It was this wounded sense of self that my Tibetan teachers recognized and were at first somewhat at a loss to address. What becomes particularly problematic is that with the degree of wounding we have in the West, it has become normal to be self-preoccupied and solely oriented to personal gain and personal gratification at the expense of others. Our culture seems to see the ruthless attainment of one's own needs in a competitive world as something worthy of an accolade. In the cutthroat political and corporate world, achieving and satisfying one's own aspirations for power, status, and wealth at the expense of others are encouraged. Our wounded pathology of the heart has become a cultural normality.

From a Tibetan Buddhist point of view, this wounding to the heart causes a contraction and closing around the heart chakra that cuts us off from a deep, essential quality that is innate within us all. This is a quality of mind known in Sanskrit as *chitta* (Tib., *sem*). *Chitta* is often translated as "mind," "heart," or "essence" and is a quality of mind that dwells in the heart chakra. But this is not our ordinary, worldly, conceptual mind; it is a deep quality of mind that is essentially clear, peaceful, and pervaded by a natural compassion and loving-kindness. Indeed, it is our ordinary mind, with its emotional entanglements, that closes us off from this essential heart mind.

An example of this closing of the heart was very apparent with a client I once saw. One day we began to explore the sense he had that he had no relationship whatsoever to a feeling of heart. The result was that his connection to others was problematic and left him feeling alone and sad. We began to explore this experience, and as he placed his awareness in the region of the heart, the image that began to emerge was of a dead, abandoned town with tumbleweed blowing through it. As he stayed with this image, he started to see that he never went there and that a road had been built around it because there was nothing of interest there. In the center of the town he found a desperately overgrown and neglected garden. His sense of aloneness and melancholy was coming from a feeling that even if this garden were cleared, it would not interest anyone. After some while he saw that there was a spring with water bubbling out of rocks on the hill. Despite the garden's neglect, there was still a source of life. I suggested he stay with this image for a while and let it settle in.

As we spoke more about this powerful image of a desolate sense of heart, it became clear that he had had a very isolated childhood. As a quiet and introverted child, he had felt unable to engage with children his own age and was bullied for being very bright. His pain and sadness were hard to bear, and so he closed himself off from them, shutting down his feelings. In his heart, however, he retained the feeling that he was of no interest or worth to others and so they would not come to his garden. I was very moved by the sadness of this situation in a man in his middle years.

The need for heart in our life is one that touches the very core of our sense of value and self-worth, our capacity for loving and being loved, and the ease with which we can be with ourselves and in relation to others. I recall a Tibetan teacher once saying that heart-lung disorder (a term from classical Tibetan medicine) was not something he saw in many of his own people at that time. It is something that emerges from a culture that puts huge stress on our being successful, strong, competent individuals in an alienating and competitive world. We suffer the kind of alienation that closes the heart and blocks our capacity for a natural expression of love and openness.

Time and again in the therapeutic context, the heart is a place of great pain and sadness. Returning to a healthy sense of heart requires considerable care and attention, which must begin with a willingness to feel the pain that is present there. Only when we can do this can we begin to move toward a deeper sense of self-acceptance. As the heart begins to soften its defenses and reveal its wounds, we start to go beyond the fear that cuts us off from ourselves and then each other.

The capacity to care for ourselves must begin with a sense of acceptance. If we can move away from self-judgment and self-criticism for having flaws and wounds and genuinely allow ourselves to be as we are, we can learn to have compassion and care for ourselves. Learning to value and love ourselves takes time and does not happen without work.

Opening the heart is aided by meditations that are oriented toward the cultivation of loving-kindness and compassion. Possibly the most significant of these is the practice of *tonglen*. This is a meditation practice that is particularly oriented toward developing compassion and loving-kindness toward others, but it can equally be used to develop these qualities toward ourselves. In the *tonglen* practice, *tong* means "giving," which refers to giving happiness and cultivating loving-kindness; *len* means "taking," which refers to taking on suffering and cultivating compassion.

In this meditation we visualize ourselves surrounded by countless others whom we realize are no different from us in wishing to be free of suffering and to experience happiness. We also consider that the lives of these people are often full of stress and problems, emotional and physical. None of us is immune to the struggles of existence, and few of us find it easy to live in this demanding and challenging world. When we consider those around us, there is no one who is free of suffering.

If we then reflect that whatever we experience in our life arises in dependence upon these people, we then realize that it is through their kindness that we experience happiness. In our meditation we then develop the wish to repay that kindness by taking on their suffering so that they may be free of it. In the *tonglen* practice at this point, we take on this suffering by visualizing as we breathe in that it leaves them in the form of black smoke. We breathe this in, and it becomes transformed in our heart into deep compassion. After some time we then consider the desire that those around us may genuinely experience happiness. Then as we breathe out, we breathe out a light of loving-kindness that goes to those people, bringing them happiness.[1]

If we have particular people we struggle with, we should especially place them before us and do this practice. These people are often the most connected to the pain and defensiveness we experience in the heart. For some, this is especially true of family members with whom they may have had painful relationships. The *tonglen* practice is a very effective way of beginning to clear some of this wounding within family relationships and opening up a more compassionate way of relating.

The *tonglen* meditation is a very simple and powerful way to open our heart and experience the gradual emergence of the capacity of compassion and loving-kindness toward those around us. It can also be of great value in generating that same attitude toward ourselves. I explored this with the client I mentioned earlier who experienced the pain in the heart. I suggested he bring into his awareness and visualize himself as the young boy who had suffered so much. After letting him spend some time tuning in to how he had felt and the difficulties he had had, I guided him in considering taking on and accepting this pain. As he breathed in, he visualized the pain of his teenage self coming into him. After a while I suggested he consider sending a light of loving-kindness to his younger self, giving him happiness and a sense of ease and acceptance. This he did on the out-breath for some time.

After we had done this meditation for a while, my client said that for the first time he was beginning to face the place in his heart he had avoided for so long. It was painful and sad, but at least he was beginning to feel something. He began to feel connected to himself for the first time in many years.

The heart when wounded is the source of the greatest pain but equally of the greatest treasure if we can open to it. In Buddhism the heart chakra is perhaps the single most significant area of the physical and energetic body. It is the vital point at the core of our being, the source of our vitality. The mind is rooted in the heart, even though we in the West are caught up with the mind in the head. Heart mind (*chitta*) and heart values are felt values, not intellectually conceived. They are values of care and empathy; of integrity and courage; of compassion, love, and joy. These are the felt values that flavor and color our response to the world, where we can act with the greatest integrity and care because there is a natural concern for the welfare of others.

When the heart begins to open, *chitta* awakens as a quality that can pervade our life. This heart mind brings with it what are known as the four *brahmaviharas*. These are sometimes described as four immeasurable or limitless thoughts or, perhaps more appropriately, feelings. They are boundless love, boundless compassion, boundless joy, and boundless equanimity. They can be considered boundless or limitless because they arise from a mind that is vast and spacious in its nature. They are feelings that are not bound within the ego's frame of limited narrow-mindedness, caught up in judgments and conditions. Rather, they are a completely open reflection of our care for others expressed in a way that is not necessarily directed at anyone in particular. Boundless love is the warmth of the atmosphere that holds all others dear. Boundless compassion is like the moisture in the atmosphere that pervades a caring space within which all are held. Boundless joy is a feeling that illuminates space like the brightness of the sun lightening our hearts, and boundless equanimity is like the nourishing presence of the earth that accepts all without judgment or partiality.

On the basis of these four boundless feelings, a fifth feeling arises as the heart opens. This is exemplified by the deity Chenrezig, who holds at his heart a small fragment of lapis lazuli between the palms of his hands, which is a symbol of the greatest treasure that is to be found at the heart. This is the awakening of *chitta* or *bodhichitta*. *Bodhichitta* is possibly the most significant feeling that we can cultivate: the desire to dedicate our lives to the welfare of others. *Bodhichitta* brings together the four boundless feelings with the passionate energy of intention to awaken for the welfare of others. Once awakened, it is a quality of intention that will run deeply within us like a powerful river informing the essential meaning of our life. This is not a mental intention like the ego's determination to achieve a goal; it is a deep passion in our being that moves us, one might even say compels us, to awaken for the service of the greater good. If we are willing to surrender to its undercurrent, we are taken into its power and carried along.

In the heart we find the pain and the ecstasy that are the two faces of our being alive in this difficult existence. To be open to them both is to truly engage in life with heart, with courage, and with the willingness to embark upon the process of awakening. The journey we are each on is not simple; it has many challenges and obstacles, and it requires strength of heart to be able to continue. Sometimes it is easy to lose heart and feel there is no point—that it is all meaningless. It is true that from the Buddhist understanding of emptiness, there is no ultimate meaning, it is empty, but in our relative life we need heart, we need encouragement to face ourselves and our challenges and not be swept away in despair and defeat. Shantideva, in his *Guide to the Bodhisattva's Way of Life,* says that those who become disheartened will give up and not accomplish what is needed to awaken.[2] Unfortunately, there are those of us who do become disheartened in our stressful lives when we see so much pain, corruption, and destruction around us. Then we may try to do meditation practice to find some sense of peace, only to give up after a short while—it is too difficult. When we do this, we lose heart and just return to our semiconscious drowning in the chaos of our existence. We need the quality of heart that will face the challenges and struggles of the path we are on without being blown down at the first obstacle.

Fear and despair close the heart, but when the heart truly begins to open, we will discover the natural love, warmth, joy, and passion that are abiding there. The felt quality of the heart is blissful in nature and becomes a resource to nourish and heal us when we need it. The wounding to the heart that many of us experience blocks this potential, but it is nevertheless always there if we can clear the block. The emergence of the heart mind in its most subtle state that comes with the opening of the heart brings with it a natural, blissful wisdom. This is the clear light of bliss, the innate nature of the mind in its original purity before it was obscured and closed away by the veils of pain, fear, and ignorance.

wisdom energy

THROUGHOUT THIS BOOK I have tried to demonstrate that the nature of our feeling life, far from being insignificant, is, in fact, at the very heart of our awakening. We may wish to follow a spiritual journey that is largely about the mind, its awakening, and the cultivation of wisdom, but Buddhist practice and meditation—and indeed, Buddhist life—without the presence of feeling would be a dry and unbearably dead experience. In fact, feeling is known as an ever-present mental factor, which means that every state of mind is accompanied by feeling. The deeper and more refined our experience of feeling goes, the more we begin to access the innate potential for feeling in our being that is profound and in some ways beyond our comprehension. We need to remember that the innate quality of mind is a nature of bliss that most of us have not even begun to appreciate.

In some meditation traditions it is said we should be cautious of becoming too caught up on the bliss that can arise in meditation because it can deceive or delude us if we get attached to it. While it is true that we can become obsessed with trying to experience bliss, we should not diminish the significance of bliss as a natural aspect of our being once it awakens. Lama Yeshe once said that the problem with bliss is that we can turn it into excitement and it then becomes just more worldly attachment. He also said that one of our problems is that we don't really understand how to enjoy ourselves. We don't know how to be with bliss. But it is not so much the bliss that is the problem but the way we relate to it. Bliss without a deep capacity for spaciousness, or, indeed, emptiness, can become something that we grasp at. Rather than becoming open, we contract and turn bliss into excitement.

My having said this, we need to remember that, in fact, our present experience of feeling is of the same stuff as the innate bliss that we will eventually discover through deep meditation practice. The natural bliss of the mind that arises as meditation becomes more and more subtle has the same energetic origin as our current feeling life. As I indicated in chapter 13, every state of mind is accompanied by an energy wind that corresponds to its relative state of peace or agitation—just as the air we breathe is the same on a still, peaceful day as in a wild, tempestuous storm. The same energy wind is at the heart of all of our emotional and feeling states.

When we begin to free our emotional life, the energy winds that underlie it don't disappear: they become closer to their natural state. As we increasingly free the mind from the distorted perception of reality, the energy winds become liberated from the potential to be stirred up into the turbulence of emotion. Eventually we will experience a more and more subtle state of this natural vitality, and it will be more and more blissful. For this to happen, we need to practice a meditation like Mahamudra, where we rest in the natural spacious clarity of the mind. However, we should not separate this state of mind from its feeling component. As I said earlier, it is beneficial for us in beginning Mahamudra to rest in sensation and feeling so that the more spacious and relaxed state of mind that arises always has a felt component to it. As the mind in meditation becomes more settled and quiet, the energy winds settle, and the entire felt quality will be more blissful.

There is in this process a natural letting go of the tendency to contract into and grasp at pleasant feelings because the mind is relaxing and opening. Mahamudra cannot be practiced if we begin to grasp at feelings of any sort and contract into them. We are cultivating a subtle nonstick awareness that allows whatever arises to go where it needs to go, and this applies to all the subtle levels of sensations and feelings as much as to the gross ones. If we are really able to relax into this natural, clear, present awareness—the mind's innate clarity—then the energy winds will become liberated from emotional entanglements and return to their natural ease and bliss. At its most subtle level, we return to an awareness of what is known as the clear-light nature of mind. This is the subtlest level of mind, which emerges when the energy winds become so peaceful they naturally dissolve or subside like waves returning to the ocean. As they dissolve, the mind's pristine, clear-light nature arises, which has two inseparably mixed components: one is a natural clarity and emptiness and the other is bliss. While in the tantric tradition bliss is described in particular, we could equally recognize within this bliss the qualities of love, joy, and compassion. They are nuances of the same feeling.

In the Buddhist world there are those who teach that when we experience this subtle state of mind, we should then use it to meditate on emptiness so that we hold the correct understanding of the nature of reality. Another view is that as the mind becomes more and more subtle, because its innate nature is empty, that is experienced directly when we meditate upon the nature of mind itself. Whichever of these views one follows when one meditates with clear-light bliss and emptiness, the experience will be the same.[1]

Gradually, as we sustain the capacity to rest in the clear-light nature of mind, the veils that obscure the true nature of reality begin to fade and clear. We recognize that all the appearances of our ordinary world are a reflection or manifestation of clear-light mind and as such have no inherent substance. This is the view of emptiness and nonduality that is at the heart of the Buddha's wisdom teachings. Recognizing this ultimate nature of reality, we see that appearances are the play of emptiness and that the nature of the mind and appearances arise simultaneously as a reflection of emptiness. This wisdom is a buddha's experience of awakening and is the ultimate realization of the clear-light mind of emptiness unified with the feeling of bliss.

Feeling is at the beginning of our path as something to be experienced within our daily life. On the path, our feeling life is the essential stuff of transformation. At the point of awakening to our innate nature, feeling is just as present but has gone through a radical transformation. Our capacity for feeling is at the heart of our enlightenment, transformed into a radiant quality of blissful wisdom pervaded by the universal qualities of love, compassion, joy, and equanimity.

Notes

INTRODUCTION

1. Gemma Keogh, "How Do You Feel?" in *Snow Lion* 24:1 (Winter 2010).

CHAPTER I. LIFE'S BLOOD

1. According to the Tibetan tradition, the twelve links of interdependent origination are ignorance, karmic formation, consciousness, name and form, sense organs, contact, feeling, craving, grasping, becoming, rebirth, and old age and death.
2. John Welwood, *Toward a Psychology of Awakening* (Boston: Shambhala Publications, 2002), 11.

CHAPTER 2. AMBIVALENCE TOWARD FEELING

1. In his *Guide to the Bodhisattva's Way of Life,* Shantideva says:
   If I find myself amidst a crowd of disturbing conceptions

I shall endure them in a thousands ways;
Like a lion amongst foxes
I will not be defeated by this host.

(Chap. 7, v. 60)

Just as an old warrior approaches
The swords of an enemy upon the battlefront,
So shall I avoid the weapons of the disturbing
conceptions
And skilfully bind this enemy.

(Chap. 7, v. 68)

Trans. Stephen Batchelor (Dharamsala, India: Library of Tibetan Works and Archives, 1979).

2. Gemma Keogh, "How Do You Feel?" in *Snow Lion* 24:1 (Winter 2010).

CHAPTER 3. THE SPECTRUM OF FEELING

1. This map was adapted from John Welwood's map in *Awakening the Heart* (Boston: Shambhala Publications, 1985), 80.

CHAPTER 4. DELUSIONS AND EMOTIONS

1. Dalai Lama and Alexander Norman, *Beyond Religion: Ethics for a Whole World* (New York: Houghton Mifflin, 2011), 117.

2. Ibid., 118.

CHAPTER 5. MOODS

1. James Hillman, *Anima: An Anatomy of a Personified Notion* (Dallas: Spring Publications, 1985).

CHAPTER 6. THE DISCERNMENT OF FEELING

1. The five aggregates, as they are known in Buddhism, are five collections of processes that make up the individual as a whole.

They are the aggregates of form, feeling, recognition, volition, and consciousness.

2. Jolande Jacobi, *Complex/Archetype/Symbol in the Psychology of C. G. Jung* (Princeton, N.J.: Princeton University Press, 1971), 10–18.

CHAPTER 7. REFLECTION OR PRESENCE

1. Specifically, Shantideva says in his *Guide:*
   If I become angry with the yielder
   Although I am actually harmed by his stick
   Then since he too is secondary, being in turned incited by hatred,
   I should really be angry with his hatred.
   (Chap. 6, v. 41)

2. This map was originally created by Nigel Wellings for use in transpersonal psychology training in London, drawn from John Welwood's work in *Toward a Psychology of Awakening* (Boston: Shambhala Publications, 2002). I have adapted it for use in this context.

3. This analogy is from Tilopa's "Song of Mahamudra."

CHAPTER 8. LEARNING TO BE WITH FEELINGS

1. For a greater depth of understanding of the various approaches to meditation on the nature of mind within the Mahamudra and *dzogchen* traditions, I refer the reader to the Dalai Lama and Alexander Berzin, *The Gelug/Kagyu Tradition of Mahamudra* (Ithaca, N.Y.: Snow Lion, 1997); and Dzogchen Ponlop, *Wild Awakening* (Boston: Shambhala Publications, 2003).

2. For a commentary on the Anapanasati Sutra, see Larry Rosenberg's *Breath by Breath* (Boston: Shambhala Publications, 1998).

3. The approach of the Madhyamika tradition, for instance, is to analyze the nature of an object by mentally deconstructing it and coming to the conclusion that it has no inherent nature. This conceptual conclusion is then meditated upon. There

then needs to be a shift from the conceptual understanding to a direct experience. In the Mahamudra tradition, on the other hand, we are meditating in a nonconceptual awareness and then bringing in a subtle intention to look for a particular thing such as a solid, enduring "mind."

4. Dalai Lama and Berzin, *The Gelug/Kagyu Tradition of Mahamudra* (Ithaca, N.Y.: Snow Lion, 1997).

CHAPTER 9. CREATING INNER SPACE

1. *Identity project* is a term used by Michael Washburn in his book *The Ego and the Dynamic Ground* to denote the process whereby the ego and its identity grow into being through the early years of one's life (Albany: State University of New York Press, 1995).

CHAPTER 10. TRANSFORMING THE EMOTIONS

1. Mark Epstein, *Open to Desire* (New York: Gotham Books, 2005).

CHAPTER 11. PERSONIFYING THE EMOTIONS

1. Carl Jung, quoted in *The Psychology of C. G. Jung*, by Jolande Jacobi (London: Routledge & Kegan Paul, 1968), 36.

2. Roberto Assagioli, *A Manual of Principles and Techniques* (London: Mandala, 1990).

3. This technique is known as spot imaging in the world of transpersonal psychology. See Nigel Wellings and Elizabeth Wilde McCormick, eds., *Transpersonal Psychotherapy* (London: Sage Publications, 2000), 215.

4. See Tsultrim Allione, *Feeding Your Demons* (New York: Hay House, 2008).

5. C. G. Jung, *Alchemical Studies*, vol. 13 of Collected Works (Princeton, N.J.: Princeton University Press, 1983), 37.

CHAPTER 13. THE ENERGY BODY

1. C. G. Jung, *The Archetypes and the Collective Unconscious,* trans. Gerhard Adler and R. F. C. Hull (Princeton, N.J.: Princeton University Press, 1981), 209; Rob Preece, *The Psychology of Buddhist Tantra* (Ithaca, N.Y.: Snow Lion, 2006), 89.

CHAPTER 14. MOVING THROUGH THE BODY

1. Rhythmic Healing is a unique dynamic-movement healing process developed by Ruth Noble (see www.rhythmichealing .com).

CHAPTER 15. THE NATURE OF PASSION

1. Rob Preece, *Preparing for Tantra* (Boston: Snow Lion, 2011).

CHAPTER 16. HEART VALUES

1. For a more-detailed explanation of this practice, see my *Courage to Feel* (Ithaca, N.Y.: Snow Lion, 2009).
2. Shantideva, *Guide,* chap. 7, vv. 46–59.

CHAPTER 17. WISDOM ENERGY

1. For an explanation of these two views, known as *rang tong* and *shen tong,* see Dalai Lama and Berzin, *The Gelug/Kagyu Tradition of Mahamudra,* chap. 3.

Glossary

anima. A term used by C. G. Jung to describe the female archetype within the unconscious. Anima is a constellated sense of the feminine within that is different from mother. Most often she is experienced projected into relationships as the idealized aspect of the feminine men fall in love with.

bare awareness. The natural awareness of phenomena free of conceptualization.

chakra (Skt.). Conjunctions of channels in the central channel of the subtle-energy body.

Chenrezig (Tib.). The buddha of compassion (Skt., Avalokiteshvara).

chitta (Skt.). Mind, heart, or essence.

chöd (Tib.). Literally, "to cut." A meditation practice in which the meditator generates fear so as to cut through ego grasping.

clear light. The pristine nature of mind.

complexes. In "A Psychological Theory of Types," C. G. Jung defines complexes as "psychic entities that have escaped from the control of consciousness and split off from it, to lead a separate existence in the dark space of the psyche, whence they may at any time hinder or help conscious performance." Quoted in Jolande Jacobi, *The Psychology of C.G. Jung* (New York: Routledge, 1968).

disidentify/disidentification The capacity to begin to create an objective relationship between our sense of identity and our emotional states. Being able to witness emotional states rather than *be* them.

dzogchen (Tib.). Literally, "great completion." A practice of meditation oriented toward the nature of mind.

energy wind. The energies that flow through channels or meridians in the body (Tib., *lung*; Skt., *prana*).

feeling aggregate. The feeling aggregate is one of the five constituent aspects of the individual. The other four include form, perception, volition, consciousness.

Focusing. A style of therapeutic practice whereby one focuses upon certain feelings and allows them to convey an image or a phrase that describes their nature.

Kagyu. A school of Tibetan Buddhism originating with Milarepa and Gampopa.

libido. Freud's concept of the vitality of sexual energy in the body.

lojong (Tib.). Mind training. A method of practice within the Tibetan tradition that focuses upon ways of replacing negative thinking with more positive habits of thinking, thereby changing the way we experience certain aspects of our life. This is akin to the Western psychological idea of reframing.

mahamudra (Skt.). Literally, "great seal." Meditation on the mind's innate clarity.

mindfulness. A capacity of the mind to maintain an awareness that witnesses the arising and passing of experiences rather than becoming unconscious.

nondual awareness. A quality of awareness in which the split between subject and object has disappeared.

Nyingma (Tib.). Literally, "the old school." One of the earliest schools of Tibetan Buddhism.

nyonmong (Tib.). Delusion, emotional affliction.

psyche. The totality of an individual's psychological processes, including both consciousness and the unconscious.

subpersonality. A term used by Roberto Assagioli to describe the different facets of the unconscious.

tantra. The esoteric or mystical system of Buddhist practice, which utilizes practices of visualization and mantra to transform the energy of the emotions and awaken our innate Buddha nature.

tonglen (Tib.). Literally, "taking and giving." A meditation for generating compassion and loving-kindness.

tsorwa (Tib.). Feeling, a term that combines sensation and feeling in the body. This Tibetan term is the closest to the English word *feeling*. It refers to the aggregate of feeling and is a felt experience in the body that includes both sensation and feeling.

vipassana. Penetrative insight—a quality of awareness that sees into the nature of reality.

Bibliography

Allione, Tsultrim. *Feeding Your Demons: Ancient Wisdom for Resolving Inner Conflict.* London: Hay House, 2008.

Assagioli, Roberto. *Psychosynthesis: A Manual of Principles and Techniques.* London: Mandala, 1990.

Arya Maitreya and Acarya Asanga. *The Changeless Nature: Mahayana Uttara Tantra Shastra.* Translated by Ken Holmes and Katia Holmes. Eskdalemuir, Scotland: Kagyu Samye Ling, 1985.

Batchelor, Stephen: *Flight: An Existential Conception of Buddhism.* Delhi: Buddhist Publication Society, 1984.

Chang, Garma C. C. *Six Yogas of Naropa and Teachings on Mahamudra.* Ithaca, N.Y.: Snow Lion, 1986.

Dalai Lama. *Essence of the Heart Sutra.* Translated and edited by Thubten Jinpa. Somerville, Mass.: Wisdom Publications, 2005.

———. *Stages of Meditation.* Ithaca, N.Y.: Snow Lion, 2001.

Dalai Lama and Alexander Berzin. *The Gelug/Kagyu Tradition of Mahamudra.* Ithaca, N.Y.: Snow Lion, 1997.

Dalai Lama and Alexander Norman. *Beyond Religion: Ethics for a Whole World.* New York: Houghton Mifflin, 2011.

Dhargyey, Geshe Ngawang. *The Tibetan Tradition of Mental Development.* Dharamsala, India: Library of Tibetan Works and Archives, 1974.

Edinger, Edward F. *Ego and Archetype.* Boston: Shambhala Publications, 1992.

Epstein, Mark. *Going to Pieces without Falling Apart.* London: Thorsons, 1998.

————. *Open to Desire.* New York: Gotham Books, 2005.

————. *Thoughts without a Thinker.* London: Duckworth, 1996.

Gyatso, Kelsang. *Clear Light of Bliss: The Practice of Mahamudra in Vajrayana Buddhism.* Glen Spey, N.Y.: Tharpa Publications, 1992.

Hillman, James. *Anima: An Anatomy of a Personified Notion.* Dallas: Spring Publications, 1985.

Jacobi, Jolande. *Complex/Archetype/Symbol in the Psychology of C. G. Jung.* Translated by Ralph Manheim. Princeton, N.J.: Princeton University Press, 1971.

Jung, C. G. *The Archetypes and the Collective Unconscious.* Translated and edited by Gerhard Adler and R. F. C. Hull. Vol. 9, pt. 1 of *The Collected Works of C. G. Jung.* Princeton, N.J.: Princeton University Press, 1981.

————. *Psychology and Religion: West and East.* Translated and edited by Gerhard Adler and R. F. C. Hull. Vol. 11 of *The Collected Works of C. G. Jung.* Princeton, N.J.: Princeton University Press, 1970.

————. *The Psychology of C. G. Jung.* London: Routledge and Kegan Paul, 1968.

————. *The Structure and Dynamics of the Psyche.* Translated and edited by Gerhard Adler and R. F. C. Hull. Vol. 8 of *The Collected Works of C. G. Jung.* London: Routledge and Kegan Paul, 1969.

————. *Symbols of Transformation.* Translated and edited by Gerhard Adler and R. F. C. Hull. Vol. 5 of *The Collected Works of C. G. Jung.* Princeton, N.J.: Princeton University Press, 1977.

Levine, Peter A. *Waking the Tiger*. Berkeley: North Atlantic Books, 1997.

Long-Chen Rab Jam Pa, Dudjom Rinpoche and Beru Khyentze Rinpoche. *An Introduction to Dzog Chen*. Dharamsala, India: Library of Tibetan Works and Archives, 1979.

Miller, Alice. *The Drama of Being a Child*. London: Virago, 1991.

Ponlop, Dzogchen. *Wild Awakening: The Heart of Mahamudra and Dzogchen*. Boston: Shambhala Publications, 2003.

Preece, Rob. *The Courage to Feel*. Ithaca, N.Y.: Snow Lion, 2009.

———. *Preparing for Tantra*. Ithaca, N.Y.: Snow Lion, 2011.

———. *The Psychology of Buddhist Tantra*. Ithaca, N.Y.: Snow Lion, 2006.

———. *The Wisdom of Imperfection*. Ithaca, N.Y.: Snow Lion, 2006.

Rabten, Geshe. *The Essential Nectar: Meditations on the Buddhist Path*. Boston: Wisdom Publications, 1984.

———. *The Preliminary Practices of Tibetan Buddhism*. Dharamsala, India: Library of Tibetan Works and Archives, 1974.

Rabten, Geshe, and Geshe Ngawang Dargye. *Advice from a Spiritual Friend*. Delhi: Publications for Wisdom Culture, 1977.

Rosenberg, Larry. *Breath by Breath: The Liberating Practice of Insight Meditation*. Boston: Shambhala Publications, 1998.

Rycroft, Charles. *Anxiety and Neurosis*. London: Pelican, 1971.

Shantideva. *A Guide to the Bodhisattva's Way of Life*. Translated by Stephen Batchelor. Dharamsala, India: Library of Tibetan Works and Archives, 1979.

Stein, Murray. *In Midlife: A Jungian Perspective*. Dallas: Spring Publications, 1983.

Stephens, Anthony. *On Jung*. London: Penguin, 1991.

Storr, Anthony. *The Art of Psychotherapy*. Oxford, UK: Butterworth-Heinemann, 1994.

Thrangu, Khenchen. *Essentials of Mahamudra*. Somerville, Mass.: Wisdom Publications, 2004.

Trungpa, Chögyam. *Cutting Through Spiritual Materialism*. Boston: Shambhala Publications, 1973.

Tsongkhapa. *Three Principal Aspects of the Path*. Translated by Alexander Berzin. Dharamsala, India: Library of Tibetan Works and Archives, 1982.

Tzangpo, Togme. *Thirty-Seven Practices*. Dharamsala, India: Library of Tibetan Works and Archives, 1981.

Washburn, Michael. *The Ego and the Dynamic Ground*. Albany: State University of New York Press, 1995.

Welwood, John. *Awakening the Heart*. Boston: Shambhala Publications, 1985.

———. *Toward a Psychology of Awakening*. Boston: Shambhala Publications, 2002.

Winnicott, D. W. *The Maturational Process and the Facilitating Environment*. London: Karna Books, 1980.

Yeshe, Lama. *Becoming the Compassion Buddha*. Somerville, Mass.: Wisdom Publications, 2003.

———. *The Bliss of Inner Fire: Heart Practice of the Six Yogas of Naropa*. Somerville, Mass.: Wisdom Publications, 1998.

———. *Introduction to Tantra: The Transformation of Desire*. Somerville, Mass.: Wisdom Publications, 1987.

———. *Mahamudra*. Somerville, Mass.: Wisdom Publications, 1985.

———. *The Tantric Path of Purification: The Yoga Method of Heruka Vajrasattva, Including Complete Retreat Instructions*. Somerville, Mass.: Wisdom Publications, 1995.

Yeshe, Lama and Zopa Thubten. *Wisdom Energy 2*. Somerville, Mass.: Wisdom Publications, 1979.

Zopa, Thubten. *Wish Fulfilling Golden Sun*. Nepal: Kopan Monastery, 1973.